SCOTCH WHISKY

GAVIN D. SMITH

SUTTON PUBLISHING LIMITED

Sutton Publishing Limited
Phoenix Mill · Thrupp · Stroud
Gloucestershire · GL5 2BU

First published 1999

Copyright © Gavin D. Smith, 1999

Title page photograph: Glenfarclas distillery
workforce, *c*. 1891.

British Library Cataloguing in Publication Data
A catalogue record for this book is available from the
British Library.

ISBN 0-7509-2116-1

Typeset in 10.5/13.5 Photina.
Typesetting and origination by
Sutton Publishing Limited.
Printed in Great Britain by
Ebenezer Baylis, Worcester.

For Ruth, whose idea this was

The original oil sketch for Sir Edwin Landseer's painting 'An illicit whisky still in the Highlands', in
the possession of William Grant & Sons. The paintings of Landseer (1802–73) were much
appreciated in mid-Victorian Britain, not least by the Queen and the Prince Consort.

CONTENTS

Introduction   5

1. Early History   11

2. The Nineteenth Century   19

3. The Twentieth Century   33

4. Making Malt Whisky   49

5. Grain & Blended Whisky   73

6. Whisky Regions: Lowland   87

7. Whisky Regions: Highland   95

8. Whisky Regions: Speyside   117

9. Whisky Regions: Campbeltown   133

10. Whisky Regions: Islay   143

Acknowledgements   156

Index   157

The exciseman – on guard.

INTRODUCTION

Whisky – or whiskey – is made in many countries, including Ireland, the USA, Canada, Japan, and even New Zealand, but of all whiskies Scotch is the best known, and to many people simply The Best. It conjures up images of fast-flowing peaty burns, fields of waving barley, and the exquisite golden colour and aroma of the spirit as it tumbles to the glass. Scotch whisky serves as a great ambassador for its native country, and for many people around the world Scotland *is* Scotch, a drink created from the highest quality and purest ingredients in a climate ideal for maturing it to a peak of perfection after eight, ten or twelve years. Both malt and grain whiskies are distilled in Scotland, and a combination of the two creates blended whisky. This accounts for some 95 per cent of all Scotch consumed.

The vital elements in malt whisky are the finest barley, peat, yeast and cold, clear water, all harnessed by human skills often handed down from generation to generation to create a truly historic spirit. To drink a glass of Scotch whisky is to drink of the country itself. In Gaelic, whisky is *uisge beatha*, which translates as 'water of life', and the modern word 'whisky' is an anglicisation of that expressive phrase.

Whisky has been widely celebrated in story, poem and song, and many of the celebrations concern illicit whisky – its production and its concealment from the officers of the excise service. Ever since a tax on the distillation of whisky was first introduced in the seventeenth century there has been an opposition between distiller and law-enforcer.

Robert Burns wrote the most famous song on the subject, *The Deil's Awa' Wi' The Exciseman*, and he composed it while still a serving revenue officer. Burns was far from averse to drinking whisky, and what better description of the spirit could there be than the 'cup o' kindness' of *Auld Lang Syne*? It was also the bard of Alloway who declared in *The Author's Earnest Cry and Prayer* that 'Freedom and whisky gang thegither!'.

Whisky is a product of its climate. Grapes do not grow well in Scotland, otherwise we might have a wine-making industry to rival Italy and France. Instead, readily available local ingredients were combined to produce a drink which would insulate the population against the rigours of the Scottish winters and the hardship of their lives.

Whisky was used to fuel celebrations and to console in times of loss. The 'wake' is by no means a purely Irish phenomenon, and it is recorded that at the Skye funeral of the Jacobite heroine Flora MacDonald in 1790 three thousand mourners drank a total of three hundred gallons of whisky. At the funeral of the Honourable Alexander Fraser of Lovat a few years later several hearse-bearers fell into the open grave, owing either to excess of grief or whisky.

Historically whisky-making was farm-based, and an extension of the agricultural year, and it remained so until surprisingly recent times. Distillation was for personal, or local, consumption, and only a handful of large-scale, urban distilleries existed until the early nineteenth century. Before the second half of the nineteenth century, and the development of blending, whisky was a drink for the poor, and in particular the rural poor north of the Highland line. Gentlemen drank brandy and claret.

Nowadays the spirit sells in some two hundred countries, from Poland to Peru. As well as providing a great deal of goodwill and a very positive image for Scotland, it has succeeded in making a serious contribution to the economic life of the country. It is one of Britain's top five export-earning industries, and distilling directly employs nearly thirteen thousand people, along with three times as many in allied trades and services. Almost 90 per cent of all Scotch is consumed abroad, with thirty bottles being sold overseas every second, according to recent Scotch Whisky Association figures. If the eighty-six million cases of Scotch purchased in a year were laid end to end they would stretch from Edinburgh to Hong Kong and back again. Whisky has become Scotland's greatest export after her people.

Malt whisky is made from malted barley in a copper pot still, and the product of each distillery is highly individual. Grain whisky, however, is the result of a much more intensive industrial distilling process, utilising a range of cereals and giving a far more neutral spirit. Blended whisky is a mixture of a variety of different single malts with a bulk of grain whisky, and the invention of the patent still which produces grain spirit revolutionised the whisky industry. It created the opportunity for blended whisky to

A field of barley.

Stacking peat, Banffshire.

become a drink for the world under the inspired marketing and salesmanship of a group of dynamic young entrepreneurs towards the close of the nineteenth century.

For many decades blended whisky *was* whisky, and when the novelist and former exciseman Neil Gunn's highly entertaining and polemical volume *Whisky and Scotland* was published in 1935, few readers could have envisaged a time when even the most unimaginative off-licences would stock at least half a dozen single malts. Yet today we take their ready availability almost for granted, and whisky has become a vital part of the Scottish 'heritage experience' for many visitors to the country, and for many natives, too.

When Gunn was writing whisky was a drink taken with soda. It was blended, and anyone with such bizarre taste as to want to drink a single malt would have needed to look long and hard for one. Gunn wrote gloomily that 'The great pity is that it [single whisky] should have been deflected to the business of flavouring patent spirit instead of to a natural growth within itself. . .'.

'In 1921', he noted, 'there were 134 distilleries at work in Scotland. In 1933 there were 15 (including 6 patent stills). Last year the number of pot stills at work had increased again. But the future of Highland malt whisky, other than as a flavouring ingredient of patent spirit, is very obscure.'

A number of wine and spirit merchants kept the malt flame alight down the years by bottling casks of 'single' whiskies for the faithful few; the most famous of these companies are the Elgin-based Gordon & MacPhail, and the Edinburgh and Campbeltown firm of William Cadenhead. Happily both are still in business, and continue their tradition of independent bottling.

To some extent lovers of malts owe a debt to the 'real ale' movement, which mobilised enough consumer influence during the 1970s and '80s to encourage the brewing of characterful antidotes to the bland, gassy keg bitters that had come to dominate British bars. This thirst for character and choice began to embrace whisky, and finally, after decades of scandalous neglect, the major distillers woke up to the commercial potential of the 'raw material' they had previously been pouring into blending vats.

It was the Dufftown company of William Grant & Sons who were sufficiently far-sighted in the 1960s to bottle and market aggressively their Glenfiddich as a single malt, building up a sales advantage over their competitors that they have retained to this day, both in the British and overseas markets.

Grant's also realised that there could be significant public interest in the process of whisky-making and the drink's fascinating heritage, and in 1969 they opened the industry's first visitor centre in a disused malt barn. Today Glenfiddich annually welcomes around 120,000 visitors, while the Perthshire distillery of Glenturret, another which developed facilities for the public at an early stage, plays host to some 220,000 people each year.

Today many distilleries encourage the public on to their premises, having come to realise the commercial value of 'brand identification', along with the significant additional income that non-distilling activities can generate. The added employment prospects are also valuable in rural areas where jobs are all too frequently at a premium. Glenturret employs just a handful of production staff to make its whisky, but up to fifty more people during the height of the tourist season.

Pure, whisky-making water.

Visitor reception centre, Glenturret distillery.

A quarter of a century ago Professor McDowall's perennial favourite *The Whiskies of Scotland* was one of the very few whisky books available, along, perhaps, with a reprinted edition of Neil Gunn's *Whisky and Scotland*, and a couple of modest guides to Scotland's distilleries. Now, in response to the growing interest in whisky, the shelves of Scottish booksellers groan under the weight of specialist volumes. There is even a bi-monthly *Whisky Magazine*, in addition to internet sites, newsletters and other literature produced by the expanding number of societies, clubs and specialist shops which have appeared to service the apparently insatiable interest in the subject.

In Edinburgh the Scotch Whisky Heritage Centre, situated near the castle on the Royal Mile, is an excellent starting point for anyone wishing to explore the world of whisky, and provides a very good grounding for 'live' distillery visits. Edinburgh's ancient port of Leith is the home of the Scotch Malt Whisky Society, an organisation dedicated to providing members with The Real Stuff. This takes the form of unfiltered, cask strength, single malt whiskies – each bottled from one individual cask. This is whisky with a detailed provenance and inventive and extravagant tasting notes, and is just about as far from a bottle of blended Scotch as it is possible to get. Were he alive today, Neil Gunn would surely have counted himself a member.

Such is the 'collectability' of whisky and whisky-related memorabilia, that the leading auction house of Christie holds twice-yearly sales devoted to the subject, where the enthusiastic and well-heeled collector may pay in excess of £5,000 for a bottle of something really rare. Maybe Gunn would have thought that was taking things a bit too far!

Whisky has made a long journey from its roots as a parochial, unsophisticated and inconsistent drink of poor highlanders to its place as one of the world's greatest drinks, and the story of its journey is a fascinating one. It is as much social as industrial history, and we are fortunate that many of the individuals and companies associated with the business of making and marketing of Scotch have left photographic as well as written records of their exploits and achievements. This book differs from most whisky-related titles in that it largely allows the pictures to tell their own tales. It takes a long look through the lens at the whisky industry, unearthing many unique and previously unpublished photographs along the way. It is, of course, best accompanied by a dram. Or two.

Slainte!

Recently published whisky books on display.

CHAPTER ONE

EARLY HISTORY

A modern recreation of a typical Highland illicit still.

The early history of distillation is shrouded in mystery, though the Ancient Egyptians are often credited with discovering the process. It is thought that successful distillation of alcohol did not take place until the eleventh century, and that it travelled to Europe with the Moors, or with soldiers returning to Britain from the Crusades in the twelfth century.

We will never be able to say just when the art of distillation reached Scotland, or who brought it, though the Irish claim that monks from their country introduced spirit-making to the west of Scotland. Certainly there were distilleries within Irish monasteries in the late twelfth century, where spirit was produced, ostensibly at least, for medicinal purposes.

What we can, however, say with certainty is that the Scots were distilling spirit by 1494, because the Exchequer Rolls for that year contain the entry '. . . eight bolls of malt to Friar John Cor wherewith to make aquavitae'. 'Aquavitae' is Latin for 'water of life', the equivalent of the Gaelic *uisge beatha*. This is the first written record of Scottish distillation, though it is likely that the practice was already established well before that date, particularly as eight bolls is the equivalent of half a ton, which means that the Friar was distilling on a considerable scale. The medicinal properties of whisky were considered so significant that in 1505 the Guild of Surgeon Barbers in Edinburgh was given a monopoly on whisky-making in the city.

The production of whisky in Scotland remained principally a small-scale activity until the eighteenth century, though in 1579 the Scottish Parliament largely banned the use of grain for distilling for a year because of a crop failure, which suggests that the activity was widespread by that date.

That bane of distillers past and present, excise duty, was first introduced by the Scottish Parliament in January 1644, when the duty on spirits was set at *2s 8d Scots* per Scots pint, which was approximately one-third of a gallon. Excise duty was subsequently levied from time to time until the Treaty of Union between England and Scotland in 1707 led to the creation of a Scottish Excise Board, since when it has been an unwelcome fact of life for whisky producers and consumers alike.

On the day when duty was first imposed on whisky someone decided to evade it, and the making and smuggling of illicit whisky was a significant feature of the industry until the mid-nineteenth century. On one hand there were wily locals who knew every inch of terrain and who enjoyed the support of most people in their area, while pitched against them were the hapless, poorly paid excisemen or 'gaugers'. That they made any seizures and arrests at all is, perhaps, remarkable, but it is certain that they only scratched the surface of the problem of illicit whisky production and distribution. Encounters between gaugers and whisky-makers were frequently bloody, and a number of excise officers lost their lives in the line of duty.

The 'smugglers', as those engaged in making and trading illegal whisky were known, were famously ingenious at hiding their stills, with at least one being set up in a cave behind a waterfall so that the tell-tale smoke from distilling appeared as spray, and in other cases chimneys were connected from whisky-making bothies to nearby cottages, where they were linked up with domestic fires. The smugglers could be equally ingenious when it came to transporting their 'make', with women wearing bladders and tin vessels filled with spirit beneath their voluminous skirts, while more than one funeral cortège provided cover for a coffin filled with kegs of whisky to pass undetected before the gaugers' very eyes.

The mid-eighteenth century saw a growth in the number of distilleries, particularly in the Lowlands, largely as a result of two pieces of legislation. Firstly, the 1725 Malt Tax – only imposed after riots in Edinburgh and Glasgow – had the effect of curbing ale production and consequently increasing the quantity of whisky distilled and consumed. Another effect, however, was that distillers began to use as little malted barley as they could, in order to avoid paying the tax, adding great quantities of raw grain instead, and much inferior whisky was produced. Secondly, the 1736 Gin Act imposed a high level of duty on gin manufacture but left whisky unaffected.

In the Lowlands two families, the Haigs and the Steins, developed a near stranglehold on legal distilling during the last two decades of the eighteenth century, with the families being united from 1751 when John Haig married Margaret Stein. It was a leading member of the latter family, Robert Stein, who developed the forerunner of the Coffey still, which was to revolutionise whisky-making during the nineteenth century.

The 1784 Wash Act reduced duty and simplified regulations regarding the production of legal whisky, as well as establishing a precise geographical boundary between the Highland and Lowland distillers for excise purposes, as one aim of the act was to stimulate legal distilling in the Highlands and reduce smuggling. Accordingly, lower rates of excise duty were applied to small-scale distilleries north of the designated 'Highland Line' which used locally produced barley, though their make was banned from being exported into the Lowlands a year later in order to protect Lowland distillers from unfair competition.

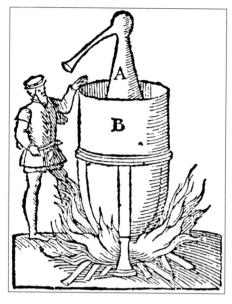

An early example of a still.

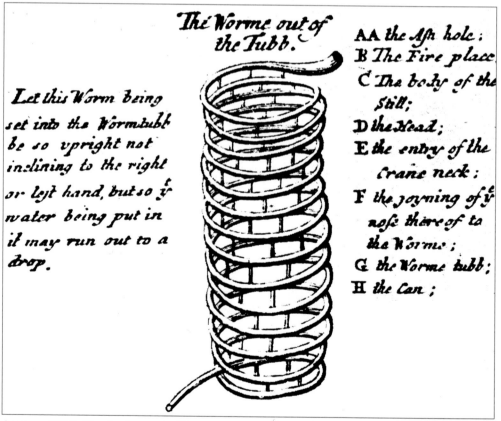

The Worme out of the Tubb.

Let this Worm being set into the Wormtubb be so vpright not inclining to the right or left hand, but so ẙ water being put in it may run out to a drop.

AA the Ash hole;
B The Fire place.
C The body of the Still;
D the Head;
E the entry of the Crane neck;
F the joyning of ẙ nose thereof to the Worme;
G the Worme tubb;
H the Can;

A worm, 1705. The development of the copper worm during the mid-sixteenth century was one of the most significant advances ever made in distilling technology. The earliest stills used air to cool the vapour, which produced low yields, but passing the vapour in a tube through water improved efficiency quite dramatically.

Interior of a distillery during the
early eighteenth century.

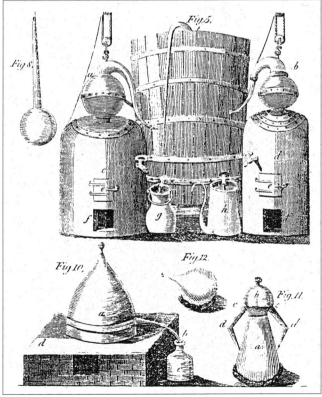

Distilling equipment, 1757,
from Cooper's *The Complete
Distiller*.

In June 1983 a party of five intrepid men and one woman, led by Perth-based excise officer Irvine Butterfield, made a 140-mile trek from The Macallan distillery on Speyside to Perth, following a network of traditional routes once used by whisky smugglers. The trip was sponsored to raise money for the Erskine Hospital, and the participants wore period dress, travelling with five Highland garrons – sturdy ponies traditionally used by deer stalkers.

Linda Wright and Peter Conroy, pictured in Little Glen Shee. Each garron carried two 5 gallon casks of whisky, which were supplied by The Macallan, Glenfarclas and Tamnavoulin distilleries.

A modern recreation of a typical Highland illicit still.

An illicit still and associated whisky-making paraphernalia on display in the Museum of Islay Life in Port Charlotte, 1994. The Hebridean island of Islay has long been renowned as a centre for distillation. This still is believed to have been used in the hills behind McArthur's Head, on the remote east coast of the island.

No. 230

WE, whofe Hands are hereunto fet, being the major Part of the Commiffioners of Excife in that Part of *Great Britain* called *Scotland*, by virtue and in purfuance of an Act of Parliament, made and paffed in the Twenty-fifth Year of the Reign of His Majefty King GEORGE the Third, do hereby LICENSE, AUTHORIZE, and EMPOWER *James Armour Jun* refiding at *Campbeltown* in the County of *Argyle* to erect, keep, and work, at *Campbeltown* in the Parifh of *Campbeltown* in the County of *Argyle* but not elfewhere, a STILL of the cubical Contents, including the Head, of *Forty* Gallons *Englifh* Meafure, and to diftil and draw off Spirits from the Barley, Beer, or Big, of the Growth of the Counties of *Orkney, Caithnefs, Sutherland, Rofs, Cromarty, Invernefs, Argyle, Bute, Aberdeen, Forfar, Kincardine, Banff, Nairn,* and *Elgin,* and of fuch Parts of the Counties of *Dumbarton, Stirling, Clackmannan,* and *Perth,* as are to the North and Weft of a Line, beginning at the Boat of *Balloch,* where *Loch Lomond* runs into the River *Leven,* and proceeding along the great Military Road from thence, by *Buchlivie,* to the Town of *Stirling,* and from thence, along the great Road called *Hillfoot Road,* on the South Side of the *Ochell Hills,* till it meets with the great Road from *Kinrofs* to *Perth,* and along the fame, till it comes to *the Bridge of Earn,* and along *the Water of Earn,* till its Junction with the River *Tay,* and along that River till it joins the *German* Ocean; during the Term of One Year, and for no longer or fhorter Space, from the Date of this Commiffion, or Licence; and to ufe, fell, and difpofe of the Spirits fo diftilled, fubject to the Reftrictions and Regulations contained in the above-mentioned Act of Parliament; he the faid *James Armour Jun* having paid down the Sum of *ten pounds fterling* being One Quarter of the Compofition or Licence Duty, at the Rate of TWENTY SHILLINGS Sterling yearly for each *Englifh* Gallon of the Content of the aforefaid Still; and having alfo found fufficient Security for the further Sum of FIFTY POUNDS STERLING to anfwer the Payment of fuch Penalties as he may incur, in Terms of the faid Act of Parliament in that Cafe lately made and provided. GIVEN under our Hands, at the Chief Office of Excife in *Edinburgh,* this *firft* Day of *December* in the Year One thoufand feven hundred and ninety *One Years*

A distillery licence from 1791 for a small still in the burgh of Campbeltown, close to the tip of the Kintyre peninsula in Argyllshire. Around this time some thirty distilleries were operating in Kintyre without the benefit of licences, and half a century later the town had become the home of almost as many legal distilleries. If the art of whisky-making came to Scotland from Ireland, then it would probably have been practised first in areas such as Kintyre and the Isle of Islay.

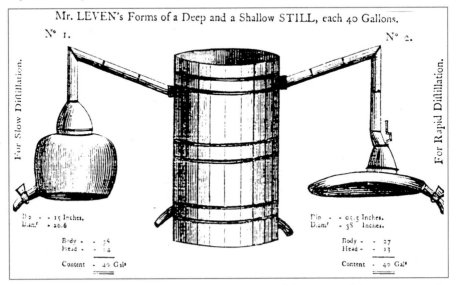

An illustration from a 1798 report by a Select Committee of the House of Commons into the state of distilling in Scotland. At this time duty was charged on still capacity. The still on the left is of the Highland variety, while the shallow vessel on the right is from the Lowland area of production. The Lowland still could be worked considerably faster than its Highland counterpart, and therefore produce a greater quantity of spirit. The quality, however, was considerably inferior.

CHAPTER TWO

THE NINETEENTH CENTURY

Glen Grant distillery in Rothes, late 1860s.

By the early 1800s there was a large-scale illicit whisky trade between the Highlands and the Lowlands, particularly as the inferiority of Lowland whisky had by this time become an accepted matter of fact. In 1816 the government introduced yet another piece of excise legislation, the Small Stills Act, which abolished the differential rates of duty and reduced the sums levied throughout Scotland. The minimum legal capacity for stills was lowered to 40 gallons, as a result of which forty-five new distilleries opened in the Highlands in the first three years following the Act, taking the total to fifty-seven.

The illicit trade was still a problem, however, but the most significant piece of excise legislation of all time, the 1823 Excise Act, was to lay the foundations for the prosperous legal whisky industry that developed during the second half of the nineteenth century, and it dramatically reduced illegal distillation.

The Duke of Gordon, a major landowner in north-east Scotland, was instrumental in setting up a royal commission to investigate ways in which legal distilling could be encouraged, and Gordon and his fellow Scottish landowners pledged to help enforce new legislation that liberalised the existing excise laws. The resultant 1823 Act reduced duty significantly, and the number of licensed distilleries in Scotland doubled in two years, with production of duty-paid whisky rising from two million gallons to six million gallons per annum. Illicit distillation fell dramatically during the next few years, with an astonishing fourteen thousand detections during 1823, but only 692 in 1834, and just six in 1874.

If the 1823 Excise Act was a major factor in the creation of the modern whisky industry, then the invention of the patent or Coffey still gave distillers the opportunity to blend malts and grains and create an entirely new kind of whisky. It was a product with enormous potential, because of its comparative inexpensiveness, consistency, and a lightness of body and flavour that made it ideal as a base for longer drinks. Had the art of blending whisky never developed, it is unlikely that Scotch would ever have found its way far from its native shores.

Unofficial blending by merchants and publicans had been practised in Scotland for some time prior to the launch in 1853 of the first commercial 'vatted' malt whisky, Usher's OVG (Old Vatted Glenlivet), which was developed in Edinburgh by Andrew Usher. OVG was a mixture of malt whiskies of differing ages rather than a blend, but Usher was soon perfecting the art of producing blends of malt and grain whiskies, and the 1860 Spirits Act made it legal for the first time to blend malt and grain whiskies from different distilleries prior to payment of duty. Usher can be credited with being the first really successful whisky blender.

The proponents of blended whiskies were greatly aided in their attempts to secure major world markets by the arrival in France of *phylloxera vastatrix*, an insect which destroys vines by attacking their leaves and roots, and which was first identified in France in 1865. During the 1880s it caused the almost total cessation of Cognac brandy production, and the gentlemen of England and far beyond soon required something else to accompany their soda. There was no shortage of thrusting, eager young Scottish entrepreneurs ready to persuade them of the delights of blended whisky, and many fortunes were made, and some lost, before the turn of the century.

The story of Tommy Dewar is as good an example as any of the buccaneering spirit prevalent in the industry at that time. Tommy was a son of the Perth whisky merchant and blender John Dewar, and in 1885 at the age of twenty-one he set off for London, armed with two business introductions, and the intention of making the Dewar's brand well known in the capital. Unfortunately one of the two contacts turned out to be dead and the other bankrupt, but, undeterred, Tommy proceeded with his aim, using a mixture of natural flamboyance, wit and sheer persistence. He also used advertising on a grand scale. By 1892 Dewar's was the foremost whisky brand in London, with the firm holding a Royal Warrant from Queen Victoria, and with the domestic market conquered, 'Whisky Tom' Dewar set off on a two year trip around the world, visiting twenty-six countries and appointing thirty-two agents in the process.

Not surprisingly, the growth in blended whisky sales necessitated a substantial increase in the supply of malt whisky, and during the last decade of the century no fewer than thirty-three new malt distilleries were built, along with two grain plants. The whisky industry has, by its very nature, always been susceptible to periods of boom and bust, as it is difficult to project the state of the market by the time the whisky being made reaches maturity. Over-supply and periods of depression have frequently been the end result of distillery expansion programmes, and the 1890s were to be no exception.

The extent of the problem of over-production during the 1890s can be gauged by the fact that in 1891–92 the amount of warehoused whisky in Scotland stood at 2 million gallons, but by 1898–99 this figure had risen to 13.5 million gallons. The bubble finally burst when the dynamic Leith-based whisky company of Pattison's Ltd failed early in 1899, revealing liabilities in excess of £500,000, which represented a very large-scale bankruptcy at the time. The two flamboyant Pattison brothers, Robert and Walter, subsequently served prison sentences for fraud, but the Pattison collapse precipitated a crisis of confidence in the whisky industry, and the knock-on effect meant that many other firms were forced into insolvency, and a number of distilleries closed down.

The great Elgin-based distillery architect Charles Doig was responsible for the construction of Glen Elgin distillery, which opened in 1900, and he predicted that no new distilleries would be built in the Highlands for more than half a century. Many of the workmen who had been employed on the Glen Elgin project could not be paid in full, and the story goes that only the steeplejacks received their full entitlement, and then just because they threatened to dismantle the chimney if payment was not forthcoming!

The ruins of the original Glenlivet distillery at Upper Drumin as it was in 1924, exactly a century after George Smith of Glenlivet became the first person to take out a licence as a result of the new Excise Act.

A bottle of Usher's Old Vatted Glenlivet. As the firm of Andrew Usher & Co. prospered, so Andrew and his brother John proved great benefactors to the city of Edinburgh, with Andrew endowing the Usher Hall concert venue with £100,000 in 1896.

Detail of a patent still at Edinburgh's Caledonian grain distillery.

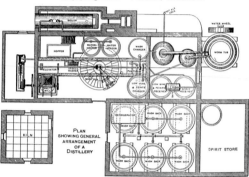
An 1887 advertisement showing a typical distillery layout.

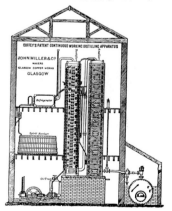
An 1887 advertisement for a Coffey still.

Tommy Dewar (1864–1930), one of the most colourful personalities in the history of whisky distilling. With his elder brother, John, 'Whisky Tom' Dewar expanded the family firm dramatically. In 1880 it made a profit of £1,321, but when the company merged with the Distillers' Company Ltd (DCL) in 1925 annual profits were running at just under £1.2m. Tommy Dewar was knighted in 1901, and in 1919 he was elevated to the peerage as Lord Dewar of Homestall, three years after his brother John became Lord Forteviot of Dupplin, the first of the 'Whisky Barons'.

An undated advertisement for Aberfeldy malt whisky. This Perthshire distillery was built by the Dewar family to guarantee supplies of malt for their increasingly popular blends, and began producing spirit in 1898.

A cask stencil from Tullymet distillery, Ballinluig, Perthshire. John Dewar & Sons acquired Tullymet, between Pitlochry and Aberfeldy, in 1890, and continued to run it even when their Aberfeldy distillery was in production. Tullymet closed in 1912, and the plant was subsequently dismantled.

THE

"BUCHANAN BLEND,"

FINEST OLD HIGHLAND MALT WHISKY,

By special appointment, as at present supplied to

THE HOUSE OF COMMONS.

SOLE PROPRIETORS:

JAMES BUCHANAN & CO.,

GLASGOW, LEITH,

AND

20, BUCKLERSBURY, LONDON,

E.C.

In Bond at Glasgow, Leith, and London, in Butts, Hhds., quarter Casks, and Cases of one dozen. Prices and samples to Home and Export Trade on application.

An 1887 advertisement for The Buchanan Blend. James Buchanan (1849–1935) was one of the great pioneers of blended Scotch, marketing his whisky in a black bottle with a white label. He later registered his brand as Black & White, and in 1922 was created Lord Woolavington. Like Tommy Dewar, Buchanan became an enthusiastic and successful breeder of racehorses in his later years, twice winning the Derby.

Early bottlings of two of the best-known pioneering whisky blends, White Horse and Johnnie Walker. The founder of White Horse, Peter Mackie, was the third of the 'Whisky Barons', though he never actually became a baron, being knighted in 1920 by Lloyd George's coalition government. Mackie's White Horse Distillers Ltd joined the Distillers Company Ltd in 1927, two years after the Kilmarnock firm of John Walker & Sons Ltd.

Early bottlings of Haig's, and Teacher's Highland Cream. John Haig & Co. was one of the six companies that formed the Distillers Company Ltd in 1877, while Dewar's and Buchanan's joined DCL in 1925, having merged ten years previously. William Teacher's was wooed by DCL during the 1920s, but refused to succumb to the giant combine's blandishments, remaining independent until 1976.

One of the earliest known photographs of Glen Grant distillery in Rothes, taken in the late 1860s. Glen Grant was one of the older Speyside distilleries, dating from 1840. As the development of blended whisky grew apace during the second half of the nineteenth century, so the delicate Speyside malts began to eclipse those from the west coast whisky centre of Campbeltown. Many new distilleries were constructed, and existing plants were upgraded and expanded, until Speyside was the dominant whisky-producing region by the turn of the century.

A page from William Grant of Glenfiddich's first cash book. It includes a payment of £102 9s 7d to Mrs Cumming of Cardow for distilling equipment, along with 1s for paper for the plans of Glenfiddich distillery in Dufftown, from which spirit first flowed on Christmas Day of 1887.

Loading casks of Glen Grant on to a train belonging to the Great North of Scotland Railway at Rothes station in 1892. As the railway network developed in Britain during the second half of the nineteenth century new distilleries tended to be built close to lines, in order to facilitate the import of raw materials, such as coal and barley, and the export of casks of spirit. The Great North of Scotland Railway operated trains between Keith and Boat of Garten, near Aviemore, with a branch line via Rothes to Elgin, and therefore served many Speyside distilleries, linking them to Perth, Edinburgh and England.

Dailuaine distillery's 'puggie' engine. Many distilleries had their own puggies, which ran between the plants' private sidings and the public rail network. The Dailuaine engine has been preserved, and is now on display at Aberfeldy distillery.

An advertisement from the 1880s for Roderick Dhu blended whisky. For many years Wright & Greig relied on Highland Park as a principal malt for Roderick Dhu, but by the 1890s their blend was one of the most popular in Britain, and in 1900 they acquired the newly opened Dallas Dhu distillery near Forres on Speyside. Dallas Dhu was designed by Charles Doig, and is now a 'distillery museum' in the care of Historic Scotland.

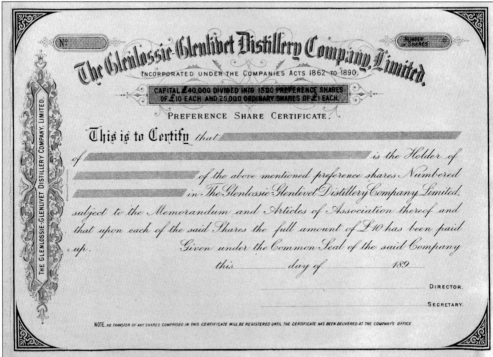

Share certificate relating to Glenlossie distillery, 1895. Glenlossie was built near Elgin in 1876, and was incorporated as the Glenlossie-Glenlivet Distillery Company Limited in 1895. A controlling interest was acquired by the DCL subsidiary Scottish Malt Distillers Ltd in 1919, and DCL took complete control eleven years later.

Charles Doig (1855–1918), one of the most prolific and influential distillery architects of all time. The work of Doig is still evident in many distilleries throughout Scotland, and he created that most distinctive of distillery features, the malt kiln pagoda roof.

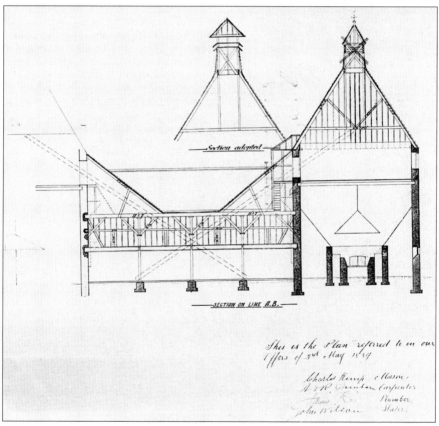

One of Doig's plans for development work on Dailluaine distillery, near Aberlour, in May 1889. The drawing shows his first intention, a chimney with slatted sides, clearly crossed out, with the innovative pagoda-shaped alternative alongside. Not only did the new design look attractive, but it also gave a stronger draw to the furnace below, and Doig's new feature was soon in great demand. Kilns were first built with tapering roofs capped with ventilators in the 1750s, in order to draw heat more efficiently through the drying floor.

An advertisement for Pattison's whisky, from the 1890s. The militaristic theme is typical of much advertising of the time. A factor in Pattison's downfall was the company's over-indulgence in extravagant promotion. One of its marketing initiatives consisted of training hundreds of grey parrots to say 'Drink Pattison's Whisky'!

Another advert that relied on the patriotic fervour of the British at war in order to sell whisky. This one is much more specific than the Pattison example, though whether the Pretoria prison camp was really such a centre of indiscriminate conviviality remains a matter of conjecture.

CHAPTER THREE

THE TWENTIETH CENTURY

Drawing cask samples of Benrinnes malt for analysis by the excise officer,
Inveralmond, Perth, 1962.

As sales of blended whisky rose dramatically during the last two decades of the nineteenth century there was an increase in the amount of very poor quality, and frequently adulterated, spirit that found its way on to the market. Much whisky sold as 'malt' was, in fact, nothing of the kind. This caused widespread concern, and the Scottish Malt Distillers Association sought to protect the reputation of their product by insisting that only the malt product of pot stills should be sold as Scotch whisky. In 1906 Islington Borough Council in north London charged a publican and off-licence trader with selling as malt whisky a product which was proven to be 90 per cent grain spirit, and the 'What is Whisky?' case had begun. In 1908–9 a Royal Commission of Inquiry pontificated on the matter, effectively finding in favour of the blenders and grain distillers, and rejecting the call for a compulsory bonding period for all whiskies. The Commission concluded: 'We are unable to recommend that the use of the word "whisky" should be restricted to spirit manufactured by the pot-still process.' This was great news for the blenders, and for the Distillers Company Ltd in particular, as they had lobbied hard for such a result. A minimum bonding period of two years was finally introduced by Lloyd George in the Immature Spirits Act of 1915, and the following year this was extended to three years, the period still in force today. Lloyd George's legislation had more to do with curbing the prevailing drunkenness among munition workers and a desire to see an overall reduction in drinking rather than any concern for the integrity of the spirit itself. Indeed, as Chancellor of the Exchequer, Lloyd George had proved himself no friend to the distilling industry when he increased duty by one-third in his 'People's Budget' of 1909.

Charles Doig was proved correct in his gloomy pre-millennial prediction that no new Highland distilleries would be constructed during the first half of the twentieth century, with two world wars, United States alcohol prohibition and the inter-war depression all conspiring to keep the Scotch whisky business in the doldrums. Prohibition did not, however, mean an end to the trade in Scotch whisky between Britain and the USA, and whisky found its way into America by many devious routes. The ingenuity that had served the smugglers of old so well resurfaced, with supplies of whisky even being loaded into torpedoes and fired on to US beaches from motor boats anchored offshore!

Maritime adventures were also central to the most famous whisky-related novel of all time. *Whisky Galore* was written by Compton – later Sir Compton – Mackenzie, and published in 1947. It was subsequently made into a successful film, starring James Robertson Justice, Joan Greenwood and Gordon Jackson. Mackenzie lived for many years on the Hebridean island of Barra, where he wrote *Whisky Galore*, and in later life he was to claim that the hardest part of writing the novel was rendering factual aspects of the situation believable in fiction. The book was inspired by real-life events which followed the wrecking of the SS *Politician* off the island of Eriskay, near Barra, in August 1941, while carrying a cargo of Scotch whisky to the USA. Subsequently islanders helped themselves to a significant part of the cargo, and bottles were ingeniously hidden in gutterings, haystacks and babies' cots.

The first new distillery to be built in the Highlands in the twentieth century was Tormore, which was constructed between 1958 and 1960 at Advie, near Grantown-on-Spey for Long John International, and architecturally speaking, it was worth the wait. Tormore was designed by Sir Albert Richardson, and remains a showpiece distillery. Between 1959 and 1966 malt whisky production rose from 16 million gallons per annum to 51 million gallons, with some distilleries being brought out of mothballs, while many more were significantly expanded and upgraded. Other new Speyside distilleries followed Tormore, including Glenallachie, near Aberlour, and another showpiece plant in the shape of Auchroisk, at Mulben.

The historical sequence of the 1890s was to be repeated, however, as the end of the 1970s saw a decline in whisky sales in Britain and the USA, and the onset of a world-wide economic recession, which blighted new-found export opportunities. The Distillers' Company Ltd closed eleven of its forty-five malt distilleries in 1983, followed by a further ten two years later. In all, twenty-nine distilleries fell silent during the first half of the 1980s, as producers sought to lower the levels of the international 'whisky loch'.

Reflecting industry in general, ownership of distilleries has become concentrated into fewer and fewer hands, with the Canadian Seagram company being an early foreign investor in Scotch whisky, acquiring Strathisla distillery in 1950, and building a significant power-base on Speyside. Fellow Canadian distillers Hiram Walker had played a major role in Scottish distilling since just before the Second World War, purchasing Miltonduff and Glenburgie distilleries in 1937, then constructing Dumbarton distillery the following year. More recently Japanese companies have become important players in the whisky industry in Scotland. Guinness took over Perth-based Arthur Bell & Sons Ltd in 1986, and the following year acquired DCL amid much controversy, naming the vast new spirits operation United Distillers plc. In 1998 Guinness merged with its greatest competitor, Grand Metropolitan, to create Diageo, the largest drinks company in the world. Its spirits division trades under the name United Distillers & Vintners, or UDV.

Although recession among Far Eastern economies during the late 1990s hit many whisky companies hard, three new malt distilleries opened during the decade, and in 1999 a total of eighty-six Scottish malt distilleries were in production, along with eight grain whisky plants. The profile of whisky, and in particular malt whisky, has never been higher.

A 1906 press advertisement for Cambus patent still grain whisky. During the 'What is Whisky?' case DCL marketed Cambus energetically. Note the mischievous 'Cambus is not a Pot Still Whisky', and the slogan, unsustainable in these days of an Advertising Standards Authority, 'Not a Headache in a Gallon'.

Charles Gordon in India, 1909. Charles Gordon married William Grant's daughter, Isabella, and became the first salesman for William Grant & Sons. It took Charles Gordon 180 calls before he made his first sale, but his persistence was rewarded, and having established a sound domestic base, like Tommy Dewar before him, Gordon turned his attention overseas. In 1909–10 he visited India, Malaya, Australia and New Zealand, and by 1914 Grant's had established sixty agencies in thirty different countries.

Fire practice at Pulteney distillery, Wick, in the early 1920s. Fire was an ever-present threat in distilleries and whisky warehouses, and the histories of many distilleries, including Banff, Dallas Dhu, Talisker and Dalwhinnie, feature serious fires.

A major fire at Hill Thomson & Co. Ltd's principal bonded warehouse in Quality Street, Leith, 1955. Hill Thomson was best known for its Queen Anne blend, and 100,000 gallons of matured whisky were lost in the blaze.

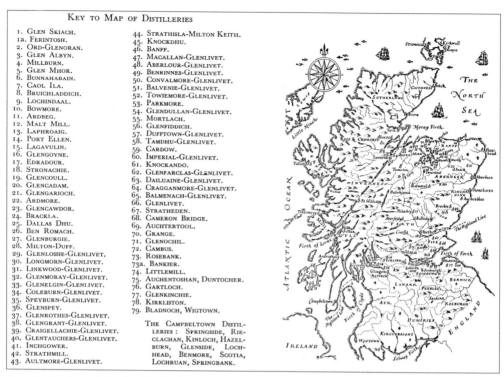

KEY TO MAP OF DISTILLERIES

1. GLEN SKIACH.
1a. FERINTOSH.
2. ORD-GLENORAN.
3. GLEN ALBYN.
4. MILLBURN.
5. GLEN MHOR.
6. BUNNAHABAIN.
7. CAOL ILA.
8. BRUICHLADDICH.
9. LOCHINDAAL.
10. BOWMORE.
11. ARDBEG.
12. MALT MILL.
13. LAPHROAIG.
14. PORT ELLEN.
15. LAGAVULIN.
16. GLENGOYNE.
17. EDRADOUR.
18. STRONACHIE.
19. GLENCOULL.
20. GLENCADAM.
21. GLENGARIOCH.
22. ARDMORE.
23. GLENCAWDOR.
24. BRACKLA.
25. DALLAS DHU.
26. BEN ROMACH.
27. GLENBURGIE.
28. MILTON-DUFF.
29. GLENLOSSIE-GLENLIVET.
30. LONGMORN-GLENLIVET.
31. LINKWOOD-GLENLIVET.
32. GLENMORAY-GLENLIVET.
33. GLENELGIN-GLENLIVET.
34. COLEBURN-GLENLIVET.
35. SPEYBURN-GLENLIVET.
36. GLENSPEY.
37. GLENROTHES-GLENLIVET.
38. GLENGRANT-GLENLIVET.
39. CRAIGELLACHIE-GLENLIVET.
40. GLENTAUCHERS-GLENLIVET.
41. INCHGOWER.
42. STRATHMILL.
43. AULTMORE-GLENLIVET.

44. STRATHISLA-MILTON KEITH.
45. KNOCKDHU.
46. BANFF.
47. MACALLAN-GLENLIVET.
48. ABERLOUR-GLENLIVET.
49. BENRINNES-GLENLIVET.
50. CONVALMORE-GLENLIVET.
51. BALVENIE-GLENLIVET.
52. TOWIEMORE-GLENLIVET.
53. PARKMORE.
54. GLENDULLAN-GLENLIVET.
55. MORTLACH.
56. GLENFIDDICH.
57. DUFFTOWN-GLENLIVET.
58. TAMDHU-GLENLIVET.
59. CARDOW.
60. IMPERIAL-GLENLIVET.
61. KNOCKANDO.
62. GLENFARCLAS-GLENLIVET.
63. DAILUAINE-GLENLIVET.
64. CRAGGANMORE-GLENLIVET.
65. BALMENACH-GLENLIVET.
66. GLENLIVET.
67. STRATHEDEN.
68. CAMERON BRIDGE.
69. AUCHTERTOOL.
70. GRANGE.
71. GLENOCHIL.
72. CAMBUS.
73. ROSEBANK.
73a. BANKIER.
74. LITTLEMILL.
75. AUCHENTOSHAN, DUNTOCHER.
76. GARTLOCH.
77. GLENKINCHIE.
78. KIRKLISTON.
79. BLADNOCH, WIGTOWN.

THE CAMPBELTOWN DISTIL-
LERIES : SPRINGSIDE, RIE-
CLACHAN, KINLOCH, HAZEL-
BURN, GLENSIDE, LOCH-
HEAD, BENMORE, SCOTIA,
LOCHRUAN, SPRINGBANK.

The distribution of Scotland's distilleries in the late 1920s. Note the preponderance of 'Glenlivet' suffixes among the Speysides, and the existence of ten distilleries in Campbeltown.

Bottlings of single malts by Matthew Gloag & Sons, 1906–26. At a time when many distillers did not bottle their own produce, the Perth firm of Matthew Gloag & Sons, proprietors of The Famous Grouse blend, was one company which offered the public a variety of malts using their standard label, over-printed with details of each bottling.

Whisky Galore author Sir Compton Mackenzie (1883–1972) at a Savoy Hotel reception in London in 1957 to launch William Grant & Sons' now famous triangular bottle, the work of the eminent modernist designer Hans Schleger. With Mackenzie is Gordon Grant, a grandson of the firm's founder, and company chairman at the time of the launch.

Some bottles of whisky from the SS *Politician* survive, and tend to fetch high prices at auction. This bottle was one of a number salvaged from the wreck in the early 1990s, and in the photograph is being tested to determine its strength. The test revealed that virtually no loss of strength had occurred during the half century the bottle had spent underwater.

Tormore distillery, 1998. Tormore is a bold, confident architectural statement, which sits well among its older and more traditional Speyside neighbours. Since 1990 it has belonged to Allied Distillers. Tormore is situated at the foot of the Cromdale Hills, between Grantown-on-Spey and Bridge of Avon. Although Glen Keith distillery in Keith opened a year before Tormore was established, the latter can claim to be the first totally new distillery to be constructed in the Highlands during the twentieth century, as Glen Keith was rebuilt using elements of a derelict mill.

Glen Keith distillery. The Canadian Seagram company bought an old oatmeal mill just across the River Isla from their Strathisla distillery in the Speyside town of Keith, and proceeded to create the Glen Keith distillery, which became operational in 1958. Seagram had acquired Strathisla distillery in 1950, and by the end of the 1970s the company owned nine Speyside plants, including Glen Grant and The Glenlivet. It now trades as the Chivas-Glenlivet Group.

A display of Queen Anne whisky in Greece (undated). The process of making Scotch whisky a drink for the world, begun in the late nineteenth century, has continued ever since.

Allt a Bhainne, one of two new Speyside distilleries built by Seagram during the 1970s. Allt a Bhainne came on stream in 1975, two years after Braes of Glenlivet (now called Braeval), and is stunningly situated a few miles from Dufftown on the southern slopes of Ben Rinnes. Allt a Bhainne was built to the same basic design as Braes of Glenlivet, but whereas the first of the new plants was equipped with a cosmetic pagoda, the pretence of maltings was dropped for Allt a Bhainne.

The heart of a modern distillery, Allt a Bhainne, 1977. Allt a Bhainne is highly automated, and can be operated by one man per shift. All spirit produced is tankered away to Chivas' vast bonding complex at Keith, where it is filled into casks for maturation. The distillery has a capacity of 1 million gallons.

HRH Prince Philip visiting Glenfiddich distillery in November 1974, as part of the celebrations to mark the centenary of the Malt Distillers Association of Scotland. Alongside HRH is Duncan Stuart, manager of Glenfiddich and Balvenie distilleries. The British Royal Family has long taken an interest in the Scotch whisky industry, with King George IV reputedly drinking only illicit Glenlivet, while Queen Victoria was once observed by Prime Minister Gladstone adding whisky to her glass of claret.

HRH Prince Charles sampling Laphroaig during a visit to the Islay distillery in 1994. The visit marked the Prince's award of a Royal Warrant to Laphroaig, the only single malt ever to have received this honour.

A 'customs' or 'crown' lock at Glenfiddich distillery. Such locks were a traditional sight in Scottish distilleries. They secured every point where spirit could be accessed, and within each lock was a space for the Customs & Excise officer to insert a signed and dated paper label. Any damage to the paper indicated that the lock had been tampered with.

Drawing cask samples of Benrinnes malt for analysis by the excise officer, Inveralmond, Perth, 1962. Before 1983 every distillery was allocated its own officer or officers, but the introduction of a policy of 'self-policing' means that distillery managers are now responsible for measuring all yields and submitting returns to Customs & Excise regarding the amounts of wash and spirit produced.

Opening of the visitor centre, Glenfiddich distillery, 1969. William Grant & Sons were the first distillers actively to encourage visitors to their distilleries. In 1969 Mrs E.L. Roberts, a granddaughter of William Grant, opened a new reception centre at Glenfiddich, watched by (left to right) Sandy Grant Gordon, Managing Director, Eric Roberts, Chairman, and David Grant, Glenfiddich Brand Manager.

Expansion at Glenfiddich distillery, Dufftown, 1971–72. Glenfiddich now boasts thirty stills in two stillhouses, but despite increased demand for whisky the shape and size of the stills have never been changed.

Casks ready for filling, Aultmore distillery, near Keith, 1924. Aultmore dates from 1895, but was bought by John Dewar & Sons for £20,000 in 1923, and subsequently passed to DCL. Along with Aberfeldy, Craigellachie and Royal Brackla, it is one of four distilleries bought by Bacardi-Martini from the newly created UDV in 1998. Aultmore is located in an area once renowned for illicit distilling.

Aultmore distillery, 1998. While in the possession of DCL, Aultmore was completely rebuilt during 1970–1, in the aesthetically unappealing style favoured at the time. As pressure mounted during the 1960s and '70s to produce ever more spirit, distilleries were enlarged and reconstructed, but much fine architecture was lost along the way. Existing buildings were frequently demolished to make way for quickly erected structures which were not always so easy on the eye as their predecessors had been.

Tomatin distillery in Inverness-shire, 1998. Tomatin was the first Scottish distillery to become wholly owned by a Japanese company, being acquired in 1986 by Takara Shuzo & Okura. Tomatin was expanded on a dramatic scale between the mid-1950s and mid-1970s, and has a capacity of 5 million proof gallons per annum, though it has never produced at optimum capacity. It is now the second-largest distillery in the world, eclipsed only by Hakushu distillery in Japan, owned by the world's biggest distilling company, Suntory.

Bowmore distillery on the island of Islay. Since 1994 its operating company, Morrison Bowmore Distillers Ltd, has been owned by Suntory.

Banff distillery in the early 1920s. Built in 1863, Banff was one of eleven distilleries closed by DCL in 1983. It was subsequently demolished, and no trace now remains.

'Whisky tourism' has become an important part of the distilling industry. The Scotch Whisky Heritage Centre in Edinburgh makes a good starting point for anyone wishing to discover more about Scotland's national drink.

The barrel ride, Scotch Whisky Heritage Centre. One attraction of the centre is a tour through three centuries of Scotch whisky history in electronically driven barrel-cars, featuring life-like figures, aromas and sounds. Such is the overseas interest in Scotch whisky that tours are available in eight languages.

Edinburgh shop window display of whiskies, 1977. Outside the capital and major tourist areas the selection of single malt whiskies was still comparatively limited at that date. The prices displayed, however, invoke a sense of nostalgia.

Loch Fyne Whiskies, Inveraray, Argyll, 1998. With the recent growth of interest in all aspects of whisky, and particularly in single malts, specialist outlets such as Loch Fyne Whiskies have sprung up around Scotland, offering retail and mail order services to all parts of the world.

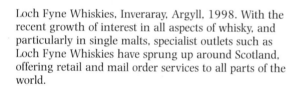

CHAPTER FOUR

MAKING MALT WHISKY

The Glenlivet stillhouse, c. 1980.

The process of producing single malt whisky has, in essence, changed little through the centuries, and still owes much to the skills of the individuals charged with making it. One of the great joys of malt whiskies is their individuality, and the make of no two distilleries is ever the same. While it is possible to copy production equipment and methods, use the same water source, barley and yeasts, and mature for the same duration in the same kind of casks within the same micro-climate, the result will always be distinctly different spirits. An enormous amount of money has been invested in the search for a definitive scientific evaluation of the variables in malt whisky making, but an element of mystery remains.

In essence, the production of malt whisky requires barley, peat, yeast and water. Traditionally distillers favour soft water, rising through peat and flowing over granite, though some excellent whiskies are made using hard water that never encounters peat or granite. What is essential in whisky water is purity and consistency of supply. The peatiness or otherwise of the process water used will be one factor determining the peatiness of the final whisky.

Malt whisky-making begins by malting the barley in order to induce germination. In a traditional maltings the barley is steeped in water for two or three days, then spread on a malting floor, where rootlets develop as germination begins. Now, however, this labour-intensive process has been largely mechanised and centralised into major maltings, and traditional distillery-based floor-malting is carried on at just a handful of distilleries in Scotland, including Balvenie on Speyside, Highland Park on Orkney, and Bowmore and Laphroaig on the Isle of Islay.

So that the malt retains the sugars essential for fermentation, the partially germinated green malt (as it is known) is transferred to a kiln after some seven days and dried over a fire or by jets of hot air, with peat used to impart flavour. The amount of peat used during kilning has a major influence on the character of the finished whisky, and many Islay malts, for example, are quite heavily peated in the kiln. The most modern maltings do not even have a kiln, however, as a machine was developed during the 1980s that embraces all the steeping, germination and kilning processes.

Once dried, the malt is ground in a mill to produce grist, after which the process of mashing begins. The grist is mixed with hot water in large mash tuns to extract fermentable sugars, and the sweet liquid which results from mashing is known as wort. What is left behind is called draff.

The wort is pumped from the mash tuns into large washbacks, where yeast is added in order to promote fermentation and create alcohol. The end product of fermentation is a liquor known as wash, and at this point the business of distillation begins. So far, the processes of whisky-making have been similar to those used to brew beer, but now the wash is transferred into copper wash stills, where it is brought to the boil. Alcohol boils at a lower temperature than water, so the alcohol vapours rise from the still first, and are condensed into liquid when they pass through pipes in tanks filled with cold water.

The alcohol produced needs to be re-distilled in order to obtain the pure spirit that will mature into whisky, and this takes place in smaller vessels, known as spirit stills.

The heating process is repeated, but this time the early distillation, called foreshots, is too strong and impure to be used, and is piped into a low wines charger to be re-distilled later. The last flow from the still is the feints, which is too weak and impure to be used in its existing form, and it too is later re-distilled.

The size, shape and overall design of the stills are very significant factors in the variety of malt whiskies that are the product of Scotland's distilleries. Stills with short necks tend to produce heavier, more assertive whiskies, while spirit made in tall, long-necked stills is often more delicate. Small stills are considered by many to make the finest whisky. These are, however, only broad generalisations, but most distillers would be loath to alter the design of stills that were making good whisky, and replacements tend to be close copies of their predecessors.

The spirit that comes from the stills is known as new make. It is a clear liquid, and before it is filled into oak casks to mature it is reduced from its natural strength down to around 63–64 per cent alcohol by volume, as this is usually considered the optimum maturation strength. Most whisky is further reduced to 40 per cent before bottling, and this is the legal minimum strength at which Scotch whisky can be sold. There is also a minimum maturation period of three years, though most whisky marketed as single malt will have been matured for at least eight years, in oak casks which have often previously contained sherry or bourbon.

The residual flavours of sherry and bourbon have markedly different effects even on samples of the same malt whisky during maturation, and in recent years there has been a tendency for some distillers to experiment by 'finishing' whiskies matured in American oak for a final year or two in casks that have previously contained port, Madeira or even wine. Thus the range of variants of even one single malt may have been expanded considerably.

During maturation the clear, fiery new spirit is tempered by the effects of the bourbon or sherry, along with compounds in the wood itself, finally producing a rounded, mellow and complex whisky, which has acquired its golden colour in the barrel. Even during maturation other factors come into play and affect the finished whisky. Spirit matured close to the sea may take on a slightly briny character, and the temperature at which it is stored will affect how much bulk and strength it loses during maturation. The excise authorities who police the production and storage of whisky allow for up to 2 per cent of natural evaporation through the porous oak each year. This is known as the 'angels' share, and perhaps explains why so many visitors to the Highlands describe the air as 'intoxicating'!

Unloading barley at Longmorn distillery near Elgin, *c.* 1924. 'CR' on the leading truck is the abbreviation for Caledonian Railway.

Taking delivery of a consignment of barley at Glenfiddich, *c.* 1937. The barley was delivered by the London North Eastern Railway, either to Dufftown station or William Grant's own siding.

ate. 99	From Whom Purchased.	Despatched from		Quantities.		Weight per Bushel.	Rates.		Amount.			Remarks.
		Farm.	Station.	Quarters.	Bushels.		Per ton	Per Qr.				
l 13	Aberdeen Lime Coy	Netherton Blatt	—	42	0	56	25/-		52	10	0	
14	Northern Agricultural Coy	—	Lonmay	40	0	56	24/6		40	0	0	
14	D: D:	—	Turiff	31	4	56	25/-		39	7	6	
29	D: D:	—	Udny	50	3	56	27/-		68	0	1	
5	D: D:	—	Aberdeen	71	4	56	27/-		96	10	6	
10	D: D:	—	Inverurie	78	4	56	27/-		105	19	6	
11	D: D:	—	Aberdeen	64	4	56	27/9		89	9	11	
13	D: D:	—	Amage	32	0	56	27/9		44	8	0	
19	Mrs Turnbull	Smithston Rhynie		51	0	56						
20	"	—	—	74	0	56	28/6		181	13	9	
22	"	—	—	52	4	56						
22	George Stodart Huntly	—	Huntly	19	4	56	27/9		27	1	2	
"	William Murray Huntly	—	Huntly	6	4	56	27/6		8	18	9	
"	John Milne & Coy Aberdeen	—	Huntly	26	4	56	27/-		35	15	6	
24	Aberdeen Lime Coy	—	Pitfour	45	4	56	27/-		61	8	6	
20	Northern Agricultural Coy	—	Aberdeen	65	4	56	27/6		90	1	3	
7	D: / D:	—	Inverurie	47	0	56	27/6		64	12	6	
58	Aberdeen Lime Coy	—	Inverurie	22	0	56	27/-		29	14	0	
26	Northern Agricultural Coy	—	Amage	31	4	56	27/3		42	18	4	

First page from the 'Barley Book' of William Teacher's Ardmore distillery, 1899, detailing the sources of barley purchased for malting.

A rack of wooden shovels, known as shiels, used to turn the barley on the malting floor.

Turning the piece, as the bed of barley is known, at Benriach distillery, 1982. If the piece is not turned regularly during malting the barley will overheat and germination will cease. Typically the grain will spend between eight and twelve days on the malting floor until the optimum level of germination is reached.

A plough is used to thin the piece during malting. Benriach, 1982.

Balvenie distillery, *c.* 1910. The principal building is the New House of Balvenie, which was built between 1724 and 1726, and was derelict when William Grant adapted it for use as Balvenie distillery maltings in 1892. The photograph shows (extreme right of main building) what appears to be the cover of a belt-drive for an elevator, which would raise barley to the first floor.

An original malting floor in the New House of Balvenie, with a barley steep at the far end. William Grant's grandson, Gordon Grant, recalled working there in the 1920s, and noted the difficulty of contending with the layout of the rooms, which had not been changed when the house was taken over as maltings!

A handful of barley after germination has occurred. At this stage it is known as green malt.

Firing the kiln, Aberfeldy, 1950s. Burning peat in the kiln gives malted barley the special flavour that distinguishes each malt whisky.

The distinctive pagoda roof of the malt kiln. Today most distilleries buy in ready-malted barley from specialist companies who prepare it to their individual recipes, so many kilns are now largely redundant and are retained purely for decorative purposes.

Milling the malt to create grist,
prior to mashing, Aberfeldy, 1950s.

Mashing in at Aberfeldy, 1950s. The sparge – a mixture of grist and hot water – flows into the mash tun, where all the fermentable sugars are dissolved.

Installing a new stainless steel mash tun to replace the old copper vessel at Aberfeldy, 1995.

A washback at The Glenlivet distillery. The fermenting wash is being checked for alcoholic strength. Oregon pine and larch are the traditional construction materials for washbacks, and all The Glenlivet's washbacks are made of pine. Stainless steel has replaced wooden vessels in some distilleries, not least because it is much easier to clean, but traditionalists consider that wood may have a beneficial influence on the final product.

An excise officer examines a sample of the fermenting wash at Aberfeldy distillery, 1950s.

Cleaning a wooden washback at Aberfeldy
distillery the traditional way, with a heather
broom, 1950s. This is a highly effective but
exhausting method. Thorough cleaning
between washes is essential, as any remaining
bacteria ruins subsequent fermentations.

Washbacks at The Macallan distillery, 1924. During fermentation the temperature of the wort rises,
and the liquid may sometimes bubble and froth in quite spectacular style, though modern yeasts
tend to make fermentation less volatile than in days gone by. In *Whisky and Scotland* Neil Gunn
recalled: 'I have heard one of those backs rock and roar in a perfect reproduction of a really dirty
night at sea.' The machinery above the backs was used to drive switchers, which controlled the
fermenting wash. Before this innovation was introduced boys were often employed to subdue the
froth with birch or heather flails.

Refurbishing the stillhouse at Glenfarclas, 1997. The work took place during the traditional summer 'silent season' when distilleries are not in production. A new swan neck was fitted to one of the three wash stills, while a replacement condenser and a new still house roof were also installed. Glenfarclas boasts the largest pot stills on Speyside. The average life of a still is from fifteen to twenty years, though some survive for much longer.

Glen Grant stillhouse. The stills are fitted with purifiers, which produce a 'cleaner' spirit by removing heavier alcohols before condensing takes place. Note also the unusual mid-section of the stills, sometimes likened to a German helmet.

Glenfiddich still house, 1950s. The coal to fire the stills was delivered in large lumps, and had to be broken up by hand. Each of the two wash stills on the left was fitted with a rummager, driven by a waterwheel. These were revolving copper chains that prevented solids from burning on to the sides and bottom of the still. At this time the stills were not equipped with sightglasses, so the stillman had to judge the level of the liquid from the sound made when he struck the still with a metal weight hanging from a string.

A redundant wash still, nicknamed 'Wee Geordie', on display at Glen Grant distillery, 1998.

Glenturret wash still, 1996. Glenturret is one of Scotland's smallest distilleries in terms of output, with its single pair of stills producing about 100,000 proof gallons per year.

A stillman checks the strength of spirit coming from a spirit still at the spirit safe. The safe is a sealed, brass-bound glass tank, through which the spirit from the stills passes en route to the spirit receiver. The stillman is able to control the flow of spirit within the safe by separating the early run, or foreshots, and the late run, or feints, from the middle cut, or heart. The heart of the run is the proportion of the distillate which is of the required strength and quality for malt whisky.

Banffshire Copper Works, Portsoy, undated. In the latter half of the nineteenth century John Grant had established his coppersmith's business at Portsoy on the Moray Firth. This proved too far from the burgeoning demand for stills and associated equipment from the distilleries being built on Speyside. At the end of the century John Grant's son, Alexander, opened a branch in Dufftown. This was at the suggestion of William Grant of Glenfiddich and Balvenie distilleries, who was unrelated to the coppersmithing dynasty.

Handbeaten swan necks, heads and boil balls for Balvenie distillery, in the coppersmith's shop of William Grant & Sons in Dufftown, 1971. According to Michael S. Moss and John R. Hume (*The Making of Scotch Whisky*), 'The presence of a bulge in the still neck, sometimes called a "Balvenie ball" is usually a sign that a lighter yet more flavoursome whisky is required.'

A man door on a Balvenie still. Purchased second-hand by William Grant at the end of the nineteenth century, this still remains in use today.

New worm tubs installed at Glenfiddich distillery in the late 1940s. The vapours from the stills entered at the top, condensing as they passed down through a coiled tapering copper column, known as a worm, immersed in cold water. Each worm tub bears a letter 'G', the letter allocated to Glenfiddich by HM Customs & Excise, whereas Grant's neighbouring Balvenie distillery was allocated the letter 'B'.

Condensers from the wash still (left) and spirit still (right) at Glenturret, 1998. Attached to the still necks, condensers have replaced worm tubs in most distilleries, but work on the same principle of converting alcohol vapour into liquid.

Traditional tools of the cooper's trade. Of the many factors that influence the ultimate character of the whisky we drink, few are as important as the cask in which the spirit matures. The cooper is one of the most skilled craftsmen associated with the whisky industry.

The workshop area of the Speyside Cooperage, Craigellachie, near Dufftown, 1990s. One of four cooperages serving the whisky industry in the north-east of Scotland, the Speyside boasts an award-winning visitor centre and is very popular with tourists on the 'Malt Whisky Trail'.

Workers take a break at the original Speyside Cooperage, c. 1970. The business has been in the hands of the Taylor family since 1947.

In 1992 the Speyside Cooperage moved to purpose-built premises close to its original site. In a busy year the cooperage can make some 65,000 casks from new, and repair and reconstruct a further 80,000. The most popular cask sizes used in the whisky industry are the barrel (40 gallons, 180 litres), the hogshead (55 gallons, 250 litres) and the butt (108 gallons, 490 litres).

Coopers serve a four year apprenticeship, at the end of which a messy initiation ceremony dating back five hundred years takes place. Happily for the newly qualified cooper, the occasion culminates in a dram.

Empty casks, The Glenlivet distillery.

Whisky has an enviable reputation as an 'environment friendly' product, and for many years the Scotch whisky industry has been at the forefront of responsible handling of by-products. In this undated photograph pot ale – the residue in the wash still after the initial distillation had taken place – is being spread as fertiliser on land near Longmorn distillery, which is visible in the background.

The 'draff lorry' at Aberfeldy distillery, 1980s. Draff is the high-protein spent grist that remains after mashing. It makes excellent cattle feed.

The Glenlivet dark grains plant soon after opening in 1975. Today draff and pot ale are often combined to produce cattle feed in cube or pellet form, known as dark grains. The process was pioneered in Canada and the USA, and first introduced into Scotland by Hiram Walker, who installed a dark grains plant at Dumbarton distillery in 1964. In the late nineteenth century John Gordon Smith of The Glenlivet distillery was recycling by-products to provide fertiliser for his fields and feed for his prize-winning herd of Highland cattle.

The filling store, Strathisla distillery, Keith, 1952. After distillation the new spirit is piped here, where it is diluted with water before being filled into casks.

At The Glenlivet distillery in 1985, filling takes place under the watchful eye of the excise officer.

Traditional warehousing at Bowmore distillery, Islay, 1990s. The sea laps against the warehouse, as a result of which the maturing spirit is imbued with a distinct maritime flavour. Before being left to mature the casks of spirit have the distillery name, date, contents in gallons or litres, and cask number stencilled on to the end. Computer-linked bar coding is now used instead of stencilling in some distilleries.

Glenfiddich distillery bottling hall, 1937. Today many distilleries do not fill casks and carry out maturation on the premises. Instead, the 'new make' is tankered to centralised filling and storage points. Glenfiddich is one distillery that not only matures spirit on site, but also bottles its malt there.

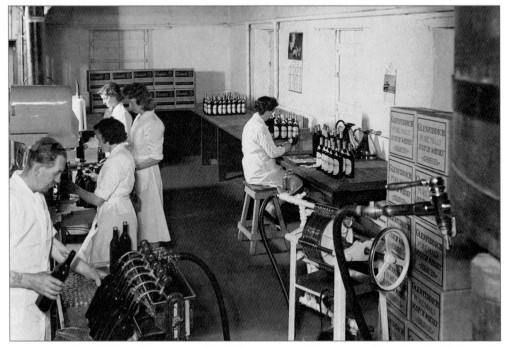

Bottling at Glenfiddich, early 1960s. Glenfiddich remains the only Highland malt whisky to be bottled at the distillery where it is produced. Note that the same man, Bob McCallum, is using the same piece of machinery as in 1937!

CHAPTER FIVE

GRAIN & BLENDED
WHISKY

Chivas' master blender Jimmy Lang at work nosing samples, 1969.

Grain whisky is made predominantly from a variety of cereals, including maize and wheat, all of which are cheaper to buy than the malted barley used to make malt whisky. The still producing grain spirit can work continuously, whereas malt whisky distilling in pot stills is a 'batch' process, requiring time-consuming cleaning between each period of production. A much greater quantity of grain whisky can therefore be produced in any given period. Because of the nature of the ingredients and the process of distilling used, the resultant spirit is lacking in strong flavour when compared to the product of a pot still, and it may be the basis for vodka or gin, as well as for producing blended whisky. Although all grain whiskies vary slightly in flavour owing to differing cereal recipes, there is not the same range of variables as in malt whisky distillation, and in theory identical grain whisky could be produced in Islay as in Edinburgh.

The processes of mashing and fermenting for grain whisky production are comparable to those for making malt whisky, but grain whisky is distilled in Coffey or patent stills, which consist of two large, connected and parallel columns, called the analyser and rectifier. In essence, what happens in the patent still is that the wash enters at the top and runs over a series of copper plates. As it moves through the still it is met by hot vapour, which separates the alcohol from the wash as it travels upwards and enters the condenser at the top of the second or rectifying column. The process is extremely efficient compared to pot still distillation. As with malt spirit, the product of the patent still must, by law, be matured for a minimum of three years before it can be used for blending, or, in rare instances, issued as a single grain whisky.

Today there are eight grain distilleries in production in Scotland, with Cameronbridge in Fife laying claim to the honour of being the first to make grain whisky. The distillery was built by the Haig family in 1824, and three years later a continuous still was installed. This was designed by Robert Stein, cousin to the distiller Robert Haig, and was a forerunner of the Coffey still. By the 1870s Cameronbridge was producing the astonishing amount of 1.25 million gallons of grain spirit per year, and the distillery occupied some 14 acres. When Alfred Barnard, author of *The Whisky Distilleries of the United Kingdom*, visited in 1886 he noted 'The Distillery is under the management of Mr Hugh V. Haig, son of the late John Haig, who worked Cameron Bridge Distillery from 1824, until 1877 when it was merged into the Distillers Company Limited. . . . It may not be out of place to mention here that the present Director at the Cameron Bridge, represents the sixth successive generation who have been engaged in the work of Distillation.'

Cameronbridge is now one of United Distillers & Vintners' flagship grain distilleries, along with Port Dundas in Glasgow. The company's grain spirit production capacity was reduced by the closure of Caresbridge at Alloa, Caledonian in Edinburgh, and Cambus at Tullibody in Clackmannanshire during the 1980s and early '90s.

Working grain whisky distilleries in the west are to be found at Dumbarton, where Allied Distillers produce grain for a range of blends, and at the Loch Lomond distillery in nearby Alexandria, which came on stream in 1994. Allied operates a second grain plant in the Gorbals area of Glasgow, which trades as Strathclyde, and is a major contributor to Long John whisky and Beefeater gin.

Traditionally grain whisky distilleries were located in the central region of Scotland, close to the owning companies' headquarters and blending and bottling operations, but two are to be found outwith this area, namely William Grant & Sons' Girvan distillery, on the Ayrshire coast, and Invergordon, on the shores of the Cromarty Firth. Invergordon was constructed in 1959, and now belongs to the US company Jim Beam Brands (JBB) Greater Europe.

Some 95 per cent of whisky consumed is in blended form, and the average blended whisky is made up of between a dozen and forty different malts, along with two or three grain whiskies. The aim of the blender has been likened to a dinner party host selecting complementary guests for his table. There should be no clashes, all must be harmonious, and the various guests should draw out the best qualities in each other. The average ratio of malt to grain is usually between 20 per cent and 60 per cent, though the more de luxe and correspondingly expensive the blended whisky is, so the higher the percentage of malt, and the greater the age of the malts included.

The legendary Canadian distiller Samuel Bronfman, founder of the giant Seagram company, declared that 'distilling is a science and blending is an art', and the role of the blender in selecting his component whiskies, usually employing only his nose, is indeed an art form. Once selected, casks of the component malts and grains are poured into a vast blending vat, where compressed air mixes the contents. The newly created blend is then casked for several months to allow all the components to 'marry', though some blenders prefer to keep the marriage of malts and the marriage of grains separate until bottling. Before bottling the blend is reduced with water to market strength, caramel may be added to enhance the colour and ensure its consistency, and filtration takes place so that the whisky will not become cloudy when water is added by the consumer.

The North British distillery, Edinburgh, mid-1990s. When DCL purchased the Caledonian distillery in 1884 fears that the firm was developing a stranglehold on grain whisky production led the leading blender Andrew Usher and a number of like-minded merchants and blenders to set up a company to build their own grain whisky distillery in opposition. The result was the North British distillery, located a mile west of the Caledonian in Gorgie. Although some ten distilleries have operated in Edinburgh at various times, only the 'NB', as it is familiarly known, remains in production.

Commer lorries from the 'North British' fleet, pictured near Airdrie, late 1950s.

The Caledonian distillery, early 1920s. According to Barnard, 'The Caledonian Distillery covers 7¼ acres of ground, and was built in the year 1855 by Messrs Menzies & Co., who transferred it to the Distillers' Company, Limited, in the year 1884. It is the second largest Grain Distillery in the United Kingdom, and in all respects it may be called the Model Distillery of Europe, as it contains every improvement of machinery and new patent known in distilling, and fully justifies this appellation. It has also the advantage of two lines of railway right through the works (the Caledonian and the North British).'

The Caledonian distillery cooperage, 1947. The Caledonian was closed in 1988, but its vast chimney still dominates the Haymarket area, and has been saved from demolition by its listed status. Much of the site, however, has now been cleared for residential and commercial development.

Cambus distillery, Tullibody, Clackmannanshire, mid-1930s. Cambus distillery was founded as a malt whisky distillery in 1806, and thirty years later it was distilling grain spirit. Cambus was one of the founder members of the Distillers Company Ltd in 1877, and grew to become one of the largest grain distilleries in Scotland. In 1993 it was closed by United Distillers, and grain spirit production was concentrated at Cameronbridge in Fife. The warehousing capacity of Cambus is still utilised, and it also functions as a filling store for tankered spirit.

Dumbarton distillery. The massive, red-brick Dumbarton plant was built in 1938 by the Canadian distillers Hiram Walker, soon after the company began to expand its activities to Scotland. The distillery stands on the site of a former shipyard, and the grain spirit it produces for its current owners, Allied Distillers, is used in a variety of high-profile blends, most notably Ballantine's. Ballantine's Finest is the third best-selling Scotch whisky in the world. Allied Distillers Ltd has its headquarters in Dumbarton, from where it runs not only its two grain operations, but also twelve malt whisky distilleries.

Architect's model of William Grant & Sons Girvan grain distillery, 1963. The Girvan distillery is situated on the Ayrshire coast, facing the island of Ailsa Craig. Far from traditional in appearance, it was the first totally integrated distillery plant to be built in Scotland since the Second World War.

Girvan distillery, as built, 1963. The site was purchased in January 1963, bulldozers moved in to clear the land in April, and the distillery was in production by December! Since the demise of Bladnoch distillery in Wigtownshire, Girvan can claim to be the southernmost operational distillery in Scotland.

Barley from the steeps going into Saladin boxes for germination, North British distillery, 1998.

Malted barley in a Saladin box, North British distillery, 1998. The Saladin method is one modern alternative to the hard manual labour of the malting floor. The Saladin box is filled with barley, and a mechanical turner moves backwards and forwards along its length. The North British was one of the first distilleries to install Saladin boxes during the 1950s, although the original process had been developed by a Frenchman in the late nineteenth century.

Mash tun at the North British distillery, 1998. In the mash tun of a grain distillery malted barley and cooked cereal are mixed with water until all the starch has been converted into sugar.

No. 2 Coffey Still, North British distillery, 1998. The column to the left is the analyser, with the rectifier to the right. A modern Coffey still can distil in the region of 11,000 gallons (50,000 litres) of wash per hour, and remains very similar in design to its earliest predecessors.

Chivas' master blender Jimmy Lang at work nosing samples, 1969.

Washing bottles at Chivas Brothers'
premises in King Street, Aberdeen,
1890s.

Taking the strength of whisky in William Grant's Glasgow warehouse, *c.* 1937. Prior to the collapse of Pattison Ltd the company had been Grant's biggest buyer, but Pattison's failure led Grant's to begin their own blending operation, based initially in the basement of Glasgow's Gorbals parish church. This inspired a local rhymester to pen the doggerel verse 'The spirits above were the spirits of love, but the spirits below set the heart aglow.'

Weighing casks in William Grant's Glasgow warehouse, *c.* 1937. Grant's blended whisky bottling operation was based for a time under the arches of St Enoch's railway station, and then in Nicholson Street. In 1960 it relocated to Paisley, and in the 1990s a new bottling plant was built on a greenfield site at Bellshill.

Disused cask weighing machine from Aberfeldy distillery, 1994.

Labelling bottles, William Grant's Glasgow warehouse, *c.* 1937. In the background on the left are vats from which the blended whisky was drawn, and on the right a bottling machine.

Casks of Dewar's White Label
blended whisky at Inveralmond,
Perth, 1962. Dewar's purpose-built
Inveralmond blending and bottling
plant opened in 1962, when it was
the most modern and productive
facility of its kind in Scotland.

Filling casks with Dewar's White Label
blended whisky from a blending vat,
Inveralmond, Perth, 1962. Once
blended the whisky is left in the cask for
a time in order that the component
malts and grains 'marry' prior to
bottling.

The main bottling hall,
Inveralmond, 1962.

Labelling whisky miniatures in Chivas Brothers'
newly opened Paisley bottling plant, 1964.

CHAPTER SIX

WHISKY REGIONS: LOWLAND

Bladnoch distillery, 1993.

Malt whisky is produced in distilleries as far apart as Highland Park on Orkney and Glenkinchie south of Edinburgh, and the Scotch whisky industry has long divided the country into geographical regions for purposes of classification. By the 1880s there were five recognised 'whisky regions' within Scotland, namely Lowland, Highland, Speyside, Islay and Campbeltown. As well as denoting specific geographical areas of production, the various categories also serve as generic terms for styles of malt whisky which are common within each category.

The first formal division was made between Lowland and Highland malts, which are separated by a theoretical line running between Greenock on the Firth of Clyde in the west and Dundee on the Firth of Tay in the east. It is unwise to generalise to any great extent about the characteristics of malts produced within each region, particularly as the 'Highland Line' was introduced for purposes of excise legislation rather than to denote differing styles of whisky, but Lowland malts tend to be light of body and pale in colour, with quite a dry flavour.

Historically speaking, Lowland whiskies have enjoyed a less than generous press. Robert Burns described the make of the southern stills in 1788 as 'a most rascally liquor'. The inferiority of much Lowland whisky was due to discriminatory excise legislation, which only equalised Lowland and Highland duty levels in 1816. Despite the unfavourable effects of taxation, however, a dramatic growth in the number of Lowland distilleries occurred in the wake of the 1784 Wash Act, and it is interesting to note that whisky was not the only spirit produced. At one time, Kilbagie distillery in Clackmannanshire produced some 5,000 gallons of gin per day for sale in the markets of London.

More than half a century after the equalising of duty across the Highland Line, Alfred Barnard was little more impressed with Lowland malts than Burns had been. Writing about blending, he noted that 'Lowland malts alone, without Highland whiskies, would be of little use; the best makes are useful as padding when they have considerable age and not too much flavour, for they not only help to keep down the price of a blend, but are decidedly preferable to using a large quantity of grain spirit.'

Legal distilling is recorded as having taken place on more than three hundred sites in the Lowland region, and when Barnard made his epic tour of Scottish distilleries during the 1880s he visited twenty-eight Lowland distilleries where malt whisky was produced. Two of the most southerly Lowland plants were located close to Annan, on the Solway coast, and a third was at Langholm. Some of the Langholm distillery survives in much modified form, while Annandale – which operated from 1830 until 1921 – is comparatively well preserved.

Doubtless because they were less intimidating than many Highland malts, Lowland whiskies were the first to become popular in England. Once blended whisky grew to be fashionable during the 1870s and 1880s, however, almost all Lowland malt output lost its identity in the blending vats, and the region has never really recovered. Even the growth of interest in single malts during the past two decades tends to have passed the Lowland whiskies by.

Both Edinburgh and Scotland's 'second city' of Glasgow lie within the Lowland classification, and it was reported in 1777 that there were some 400 stills operating in Edinburgh. Sadly for the tax gatherers only eight of them held licences! Today no malt whisky is distilled in the capital, though during the nineteenth century there were three malt distilleries in operation in Leith, along with Abbeyhill, Canonmills, Dean, Glen Sciennes, Lochrin and Sunbury within the capital itself. A few miles south of Edinburgh is one of only two Lowland malt distilleries which remain in production, namely Glenkinchie, located near the village of Pencaitland in East Lothian.

Despite a noble distilling tradition to rival that of Edinburgh, all malt whisky production has now ceased in the city of Glasgow, but Barnard was able to visit Adelphi, Dundashill, Loch Katrine (a.k.a. Camlachie), Port Dundas, Provanmill and Yoker distilleries during his researches. Of these only Port Dundas survives, and it is given over entirely to grain spirit production. However, the second working Lowland malt distillery of Auchentoshan is situated on the northern edge of Glasgow's urban sprawl, just across the River Clyde and in the shadow of the Erskine Bridge.

The historic Clyde town of Dumbarton is headquarters to Allied Distillers, who produce grain whisky in their vast Ballantine distillery complex. The company also formerly distilled a malt whisky there under the name of Inverleven. Inverleven Lowland malt is a particularly rare creature, as are Ladyburn and Kinclaith malts. The former was made at William Grant's Girvan distillery until 1976, while the latter came from Long John's Strathclyde distillery in Glasgow, before the stills were dismantled in 1975. Kinclaith was the last of Glasgow's malt whisky distilleries.

Although Glenkinchie and Auchentoshan are the only working Lowland distilleries, a number of others are currently 'mothballed' or survive in recognisable form, and their make remains quite readily available. Littlemill is situated close to Auchentoshan, at Bowling, and has sound claims as the oldest distillery in Scotland, tracing its origins back to 1772. Until the 1930s Littlemill was triple-distilled. Rosebank distillery, beside the Forth–Clyde Canal, near Falkirk, closed in 1993, and ten years before it fell victim to the accountants' decree another famous old distillery close to the same canal distilled its last spirit. St Magdalene is located a few miles south-east of Rosebank at Linlithgow, and was one of five distilleries to operate at the same time in the town.

In total, six distilleries were built close to the Forth–Clyde canal, which served to provide process water and a means of transport for incoming cargoes of barley and coal. St Magdalene also benefited from its situation beside the main Edinburgh to Stirling railway line. Bladnoch distillery, near the former Galloway county town of Wigtown, for many years had the distinction of being the most southerly distillery in Scotland. Its very remoteness counted against it latterly, however, and it was one of four distilleries to fall victim to United Distillers rationalisation plans in 1993.

Glenkinchie distillery yard, early 1920s. Glenkinchie is situated some 15 miles south-east of Edinburgh, and began distilling in 1825. In 1914 it joined with Rosebank, St Magdalene, Clydesdale and Grange distilleries to form Scottish Malt Distillers Ltd. SMD subsequently became a subsidiary of the Distillers Company Ltd. A ten-year-old Glenkinchie was chosen by United Distillers as the regional representative in its heavily promoted range of Classic Malts, giving it the brightest future of any Lowland malt distillery.

Rosebank distillery, on the banks of the Forth–Clyde Canal, 1930s. For many connoisseurs and industry experts Rosebank was the true regional classic. There was an element of surprise when United Distillers chose to include Glenkinchie in their Classic Malts range, and closed Rosebank in 1993. Given its more scenic location and its proximity to Edinburgh, however, Glenkinchie was always a better bet as a visitor attraction than Rosebank, regardless of the merits of the two single malts. Rumours persist that distilling might return to Rosebank, alongside an ambitious programme of canal revitalisation.

Auchentoshan distillery, 1990s. The site of Auchentoshan has changed significantly with the passage of time. Barnard paid a brief visit during his tour of Scottish distilleries and observed: 'It is situated in a romantic glen with a stream of water running past it.' Auchentoshan is now part of the Clydebank suburb of Duntocher. Although a Lowland malt, Auchentoshan's water supply comes from a loch located north of the Highland Line. The distillery was rebuilt after suffering extensive damage during an air raid in 1940.

Auchentoshan stillhouse, 1990s. Since 1984 Auchentoshan has belonged to Morrison Bowmore Distillers Ltd, and is notable as the only surviving distillery to fully triple-distil its spirit in a series of three stills. Partial triple-distillation occurs at Springbank in Campbeltown and at two Speyside plants, but the process was once common among Lowland distillers. It allows the spirit to mature more quickly, as well as producing a whisky that is light in character.

St Magdalene distillery, 1999. Part of Linlithgow's St Magdalene distillery has been developed for residential use, but retains its pagoda. St Magdalene was distilling by 1797, and stands on the site of a twelfth-century leper hospital.

The undeveloped section of St Magdalene distillery, 1999. Ultimately it too is destined to be converted for accommodation purposes.

A late nineteenth-century advertisement for Bulloch, Lade & Co.'s Camlachie whisky. Camlachie distillery operated between 1834 and 1920, and although it appears from the picture to enjoy a rural setting, by the time this advertisement was produced it had been absorbed into the expanding city of Glasgow.

Bladnoch distillery, Wigtownshire, mid-1930s. The distillery was established in about 1817, and operated until 1938, after which it remained silent for the next two decades. Bladnoch passed through various hands before being bought by Arthur Bell & Sons in 1983, and subsequently it became part of the United Distillers empire. As with Rosebank there are persistent rumours that Bladnoch may distill again, this time under the auspicies of a Northern Irish company that acquired the distillery from United Distillers after its closure. The distillery remains intact, and offers guided tours to members of the public.

Auchtermuchty distillery, Fife, 1990s. The distillery was in production from 1829 until 1926, and was for its whole existence in the hands of the Bonthrone family. The Bonthrones were maltsters and brewers, as well as distillers, and the family could trace its origins back to a brewing enterprise at Falkland in about 1600. Whisky made at the Auchtermuchty distillery enjoyed a very high reputation.

Duty free warehouse, Auchtermuchty, 1990s. When Alfred Barnard visited Auchtermuchty distillery he noted: 'It is built in the solid rock in front of a tributary of the River Eden, which stream comes from Lochmill and runs through the town. It took nearly two years to blast and cut out the rock, and 3,000 loads of stone were removed by the excavators.' Much of the Auchtermuchty distillery survived until the mid-1990s, when a considerable portion of it was demolished for redevelopment, though the malt barn and kiln survive by virtue of being listed buildings.

CHAPTER SEVEN

WHISKY REGIONS:
HIGHLAND

Glenlochy distillery, Fort William, 1994.

In the nineteenth century the Highland region was initially divided into Glenlivet and North Country, but the more usual split today is between Speyside and Highland, with the latter often being sub-divided into Southern, Central, Eastern, Northern, Western and Island. Because of its historical significance as a distilling centre, its continuing prominence and the distinctive style of its whiskies, the island of Islay is always allocated a category of its own. In total some 450 distilleries have existed in the Highland area. Because of the geographical diversity involved, it is much more difficult to generalise about stylistic characteristics common to Highland malts than it is for other regions.

The Highland distilleries closest to the line dividing Highland from Lowland are Loch Lomond at Alexandria, and Glengoyne, which is a dozen miles north of Glasgow, close to the village of Killearn. According to legend the line actually passes through the Glengoyne site, so that although the whisky is produced in the Highlands, it matures in the Lowlands on the opposite side of the A81. In terms of its character this could easily be considered a Lowland malt, and until the 1970s it was classified as such.

Perthshire has long been a notable centre for whisky-making, and the 'big county' still has five working distilleries, several of which merit entries in the record books, while all boast fascinating histories. Heading north along the A9, before reaching Inverness, the traveller passes firstly Dalwhinnie and then Tomatin distillery; the latter has the largest capacity of any whisky-making facility in Scotland.

The Highland capital of Inverness has grown in size dramatically during the past two decades, but in that time the town has seen its links with distilling disappear. More than a dozen distilleries are recorded as having existed in Inverness at various times, and three survived until the 1980s. Some of Millburn distillery is still extant, but the other two Inverness distilleries were not so lucky, and no trace remains of either Glen Albyn or Glen Mhor, which formerly stood on the western outskirts of the town.

Glen Albyn was built in 1844 beside the Caledonian Canal, on the site of one of Inverness' many breweries, but after periods of silence and use as a flour mill it was rebuilt in 1884. Eight years later its owners constructed a nearby distillery between the canal and the River Ness, which they called Glen Mhor, Gaelic for The Great Glen. In 1972 the two distilleries were bought by DCL, and both fell victim to the 1980s cutbacks, ceasing distillation in 1983, and being demolished three years later to make way for a retail development.

A few miles east along the southern shore of the Moray Firth from Inverness is the seaside town of Nairn, near to which stands Royal Brackla distillery. Nairn was also home to Glen Cawdor, which existed between 1896 and 1927. Continuing along the southern Moray Firth coast, Inchgower distillery stands near the fishing port of Buckie, and though technically a Speyside distillery, it is very remote from all the other facilities that fall into that category.

East of Buckie is Banff, which lies within the territory of Eastern Highland malts. Surviving Eastern Highland distilleries include Glen Garioch at Old Meldrum in

Aberdeenshire, Glencadam at Brechin, Fettercairn at Laurencekirk and Royal Lochnagar near Balmoral Castle on Royal Deeside. Glen Deveron single malt is distilled at Macduff, located to the west of the Deveron River, which divides the town from Banff. Banff's own distillery was closed in 1983, and many other Eastern Highland plants fared little better. Stonehaven's Glenury Royal, Montrose's Glenesk and Lochside, and Brechin's North Port all now figure as lost distilleries.

North of Inverness UDV operate Ord distillery in Muir of Ord, which was built on the site of an illicit still in 1838. At the time of its first licence Ord was one of ten legal distilleries in the area. DCL, as the company then was, also operated a distillery in the nearby town of Dingwall during the 1920s. For much of its existence, this distillery carried the name of Ferintosh, though it was originally called Ben Wyvis. A number of distilleries have survived close to the Easter Ross coast, including Teaninich, Balblair, and most notably Dalmore and Glenmorangie. Only two distilleries remain on the mainland north of the Dornoch Firth, with Clynelish being produced at Brora, on the coast of east Sutherland, while Pulteney in Wick enjoys the status of Scotland's northernmost mainland distillery.

The county of Caithness was home to many illegal stills, and also, in addition to Pulteney, a second major legitimate whisky-making operation known as Gerston or Ben Morvern. This was founded in 1796 on the banks of the River Thurso, near Halkirk, and, somewhat remarkably, its make became a favourite of the Victorian Prime Minister Sir Robert Peel. The distillery closed in 1875, but a replacement was constructed a decade later, subsequently being renamed Ben Morvern. It too closed, in about 1911, and the majority of its buildings were demolished just after the First World War.

The west coast of Scotland never enjoyed the same level of legal distilling as the east, and today just two distilleries operate in the Western Highlands. UDV owns Oban distillery in the busy Argyllshire holiday resort and ferry port, while the Japanese company Nikka Whisky Distilling has run Ben Nevis on the outskirts of Fort William since 1991. Ben Nevis is the most northerly distillery on the west coast, and was built in 1825 by 'Long John' MacDonald. It was the first legal distillery in the Fort William area.

The Island sub-division of the Highland classification embraces the most northerly and most westerly distilleries in Scotland. In the north Highland Park and Scapa on Orkney are still productive, although Allied Distillers' Scapa facility only operates intermittently. At one time or another there were fifteen working distilleries in the Western Isles, excluding Islay, and today whiskies are distilled on Mull, Jura, Arran and Skye.

Edradour distillery, Perthshire, 1998. As Scotland's smallest working distillery, Edradour's output of spirit fills around a dozen casks per week, or 3,500 bottles, which means that its annual production is equal to one week's make at an average Speyside distillery. Small is often beautiful in whisky terms, and Edradour has an enviable reputation as a single malt. As only around two thousand cases are released each year, it can prove quite elusive.

Bicentennial topiary distilling display in Pitlochry, Perthshire, 1998. The town's Blair Athol distillery was acquired by the great Perth-based blending pioneers Arthur Bell & Sons in 1933. Bell's paid £56,000 for the Edinburgh firm of P. Mackenzie & Co., which must have been something of a bargain even during recessionary times, as in addition to Blair Athol and Dufftown distilleries Bell's got 120,000 proof gallons of malt whisky, along with a significant quantity of grain and blended spirit.

Glenturret distillery, Perthshire, 1990s. Glenturret claims to be Scotland's oldest distillery, tracing its origins to 1775, and it now receives more visitors than any other in the country. Like many distilleries Glenturret did not survive the 1920s recession, closing in 1921, but unlike most it reopened after being acquired and re-equipped by the businessman and whisky enthusiast James Fairlie in the late 1950s. It is now owned by the Perth-based Highland Distillers company.

Glenturret's former distillery cat, Towser. Towser lived in the stillhouse from 1963 until 1987, during which time she dispatched 28,899 mice, earning her an entry in the *Guinness Book of Records* as World Mousing Champion. Towser is commemorated with her very own statue next to the distillery visitor centre.

Grandtully distillery, near Aberfeldy, Perthshire, from a watercolour of 1895. Distilling is recorded as taking place at more than one hundred locations in Perthshire, and in the early nineteenth century around thirty stills were operating in the Pitlochry area alone. Grandtully was founded in the 1820s, and for much of its existence was owned by the Thomson family. For many years it was the smallest licensed distillery in Scotland, producing just 5,000 gallons of spirit per annum.

Locally made nineteenth-century copper sampling tube and funnel from Grandtully distillery, in the possession of members of the Thomson family. Alfred Barnard wrote of Grandtully: 'It is the most primitive work we have ever seen. The whole "bag of tricks" could be put inside a barn, and a child four years old could jump across the streamlet which drives the water-wheel and does all the work of the distillery.'

Lord Forteviot (left) and Dewar's chairman Sir Norman Macfarlane install a time capsule in the 'Dewar Highlander' at Aberfeldy distillery, 1995. The statue was transferred to Aberfeldy when United Distillers closed Dewar's Inveralmond blending and bottling complex in Perth where the figure had previously stood. As the home of Dewar's whisky, Aberfeldy has become the flagship distillery of the Bacardi-Martini company since its acquisition in 1998.

Dalwhinnie distillery, 1998. The distillery opened in 1898, when it was known as Strathspey, and it is now in the ownership of UDV, who market it as one of their Classic Malts. A major modernisation programme was carried out during the early 1970s, and a visitor centre was added in 1992. Dalwhinnie is the highest distillery in Scotland, standing 1,164 ft above sea level, and the only one to incorporate a meteorological station.

Remains of the Speyside distillery, Kingussie, 1998. The distillery site is now a car park behind the Gordon Arms Hotel, and all that survives of the distillery is this range of buildings. Speyside began production in 1895, but stopped distilling not much more than ten years later, with the company ceasing trading in 1911. The site was then sold for the princely sum of £750. The worm tub from Speyside was bought by Dalwhinnie distillery and remained in use until the mid-1980s, when it was replaced by a modern condenser.

Millburn distillery, Inverness, early 1920s. Millburn was founded in about 1807, and was situated a mile from the centre of town. The plant was substantially rebuilt in 1876, and what remains today dates from that time. The distillery was acquired by DCL in 1943, and became a casualty of the whisky recession of the early 1980s, which saw such radical pruning by the company. Millburn closed in 1985, but some of the site has found a new lease of life as a restaurant.

Glen Albyn and the Caledonian Canal, Inverness, 1957. Glen Albyn's sister distillery of Glen Mhor developed something of a following as a single malt, with its one-time excise officer Neil Gunn being a particular devotee of its make. Glen Albyn, however, remained principally a malt for the blenders.

Glen Cawdor distillery, Nairn, early 1920s. Glen Cawdor was designed by Charles Doig and opened in 1896, a time of supreme optimism within the whisky industry. Optimism very soon turned to pessimism, however, and the downturn in industry fortunes caused the original company to fail after just five years of trading. The distillery was subsequently acquired by John Haig & Co., who ran it until the next major slump of the 1920s caused the plant to close once again, and in 1930 it was demolished. No trace of Glen Cawdor remains today.

Inchgower distillery, Buckie, early 1920s. Inchgower dates from 1871, and during the 1920s was still owned by its founder Alexander Wilson, who had previously run a distillery at Tochineal, 2 miles away. Although only equipped with one pair of stills, Inchgower was a large establishment, with the quadrangle design covering some 4 acres. Surplus warehousing was rented out to other distillers. Unusually, Buckie Town Council took over Inchgower from the Wilson family in 1933, and ran it for three years before it was acquired by the expanding Bell's empire, who undertook extensive modernisation. It is now operated by UDV.

Ruins of the original Banff distillery, Mill of Banff, early 1920s. The distillery worked from 1824 until the early 1860s. Its replacement at Inverboyndie was damaged by fire in 1941 when a German bomber scored a direct hit on one of the warehouses. Casks were opened and the contents poured into watercourses to prevent the fire spreading, and it is said that none of the local cattle could stand up to be milked the following morning. One enterprising fireman filled his helmet with spirit as it flowed by and shared it with his colleagues.

THE FERINTOSH DISTILLERY CO. LIMITED.
DINGWALL, ROSS-SHIRE.
DISTILLERS OF PURE HIGHLAND MALT WHISKY.

The Whisky made in Ferintosh was the Whisky of literature, and was famed in song and story more than 200 years ago. It has been spoken of in many works of fiction, and frequently referred to in London and Provincial papers as being all that Highland Whisky ought to be.

The historian Arnot informs us that within the bounds of the estate of Ferintosh, which then consisted of about 1,800 acres of arable land, nearly as much Whisky was produced as in all the rest of Scotland put together, and the barley there grown was the finest in the Kingdom. The lands having been wasted in 1689-90 through the ravages of war, Parliament, as a requital, granted to the proprietor, Mr. Forbes of Culloden, the perpetual privilege of distilling, duty free, from all barley raised on the estate. In 1786 the Government desired to re-acquire the privilege so granted, and by way of compensation had to pay £21,500—an enormous sum in those days.

During the long intervening years Ferintosh Whisky has retained to the fullest extent its ancient good qualities, and the present make ranks amongst the finest in Scotland. The Distillery, which is within a short distance of Dingwall, under the shadow of the Ross-shire mountains, is fitted up with the most perfect machinery for the manufacture of PURE HIGHLAND MALT WHISKY. The barley used is all grown in the district, and the article produced worthily maintains the past traditions of the locality for the Finest Whisky in Scotland.

SAMPLES AND QUOTATIONS ON APPLICATION TO THE DISTILLERY.

An advertisement for The Ferintosh Distillery Co. Ltd, early twentieth century. Ferintosh distillery was built in 1879, and operated under the name of Ben Wyvis until 1893, when it was re-christened Ferintosh to capitalise on the famous heritage of the name, as described in the advert.

Ferintosh distillery in the 1920s.

Ord distillery, Muir of Ord, early 1920s. The distillery was bought by John Dewar & Sons Ltd in 1923, and passed into the hands of DCL the following year. The present distillery largely dates from 1966, and two years after its rebuilding a modern drum maltings plant was added, which supplies malt to seven other UDV distilleries in addition to Ord. The whisky produced there has variously been marketed as Glen Oran, Ord, Muir of Ord, Glen Ord, and even, for a mercifully brief period, as Glenordie.

Glenskiach distillery, Evanton, early 1920s. Glenskiach was located close to the Cromarty Firth, and was established in 1896. Although it survived the First World War – perhaps because of custom from the nearby Invergordon naval base – it folded in the year of the General Strike, 1926. A major fire in 1929 led to demolition four years later, and now only some residential properties associated with the distillery remain.

Dalmore distillery, near Alness, undated. Dalmore lies on the shores of the Cromarty Firth, and traces its history back to 1839, when it was founded by the tea and opium trader Alexander Matheson. The Mackenzie Brothers owned Dalmore from 1878 until 1960, when they amalgamated with Whyte & Mackay Ltd, now part of JBB (Greater Europe) Plc, makers of Jim Beam Bourbon. The company's Invergordon grain distillery is located just a couple of miles further along the firth from Dalmore.

The still house, Dalmore, 1950s. The quirky low wines or spirit still (right) is fitted with a distinctive copper-clad cooling jacket, which has been likened to the trumpet of a daffodil. In 1966 the number of stills was doubled to eight, but part of one still dates from 1874. During the First World War Dalmore distillery was used as a deep-sea mine factory, with the result that an explosion necessitated substantial post-war rebuilding.

Glenmorangie distillery, Tain, early 1920s. The distillery stands beside the Dornoch Firth, and is built on the site of a brewery that dated back to the Middle Ages. It began to produce whisky in 1843. When Barnard visited just over four decades later he wrote that 'the Distillery . . . is certainly the most ancient and primitive we have seen, and now almost in ruins'. In 1887 a programme of renovation and expansion was undertaken, and stills heated by internal steam coils were pioneered.

Glenmorangie distillery, 1998. At 17 ft 10 in, Glenmorangie's stills are the tallest in Scotland. The original stills installed in the 1840s were bought second-hand from a London gin distillery, and they were tall in order to produce a light, pure spirit. Their style has been copied ever since. The Glenmorangie stills are not only tall but also very slender, and the spirit produced in them is delicate and medium-bodied, with a fine aroma. Glenmorangie is Scotland's best-selling single malt, and none is sold for blending.

The original Clynelish distillery, Brora, east Sutherland, 1998. Clynelish was founded in 1819 by the Marquis of Stafford to provide employment and a use for barley grown by crofters evicted from inland settlements to the coastal margin. During the 1960s DCL constructed a new distillery next to Clynelish in order to increase capacity, and the old plant subsequently fell victim to DCL's 1983 round of closures. Happily the original distillery remains, externally at least intact. Clynelish confounds generalisations about regional stylistic similarities by being sufficiently powerful, peaty, and iodine-flavoured that it could be confused with an Islay malt.

Ben Morvern distillery, Halkirk, Caithness, *c.* 1902. Three carts filled with sacks of barley feature in the foreground, while to the right casks of spirit are loaded on to a flat wagon. Ben Morvern was a particularly large and progressive establishment, with Alfred Barnard writing after his 1886 tour of the then newly built distillery: 'Owing to its position and construction the Distillery is a commanding feature in the landscape. . . . The buildings and plant are constructed on the most approved principles.'

Pulteney distillery, Wick, early 1920s. The distillery is located in the Pulteneytown area of the fishing port of Wick, just a dozen miles from the northern coast of Caithness. It dates from 1826, when Wick was at the centre of the thriving herring industry. The distillery was silent between 1930 and 1951.

Shipping Pulteney whisky from Wick harbour, early 1920s. Neil Gunn, a native of Caithness, recalled the whisky as it was when he was a youngster: 'In those days it was potent stuff, consumed, I should say, on the quays of Wick more for its effect than its flavour!'. Pulteney – or Old Pulteney as it is often known – is quite delicate for a whisky produced in such a robust climate, but its coastal location is betrayed by a certain saltiness and pungency.

Today Pulteney distillery presents a less than photogenic face to the world, having undergone an unflattering programme of reconstruction in 1959 while in the ownership of Hiram Walker, who meted out a similar treatment to Scapa on Orkney. Pulteney is now owned by Inver House Distillers Ltd, who are energetically promoting the whisky as a single malt.

Glenlochy distillery, Fort William, with Loch Linnhe in the background, mid-1930s. Glenlochy distillery was founded in 1898, and, like Ben Nevis, was at one time owned by the colourful Canadian-born millionaire Joseph Hobbs, who had made his money in property and shipbuilding and became a distiller and cattle rancher in the Great Glen. Glenlochy was acquired by DCL in 1953, and production ended during the company's 1983 round of closures. As with Banff and a number of other DCL distilleries that fell silent at that time, the whisky made at Glenlochy never distinguished itself as a single malt.

Glenfyne distillery, Ardrishaig, early 1920s. Glenfyne, or Glendarroch as it was also known, was built in 1831 and was beautifully situated beside the Crinan Canal. After he visited in 1886 Barnard wrote at length about Glenfyne, noting: 'The Distillery is planted on the banks of the far-famed Crinan Canal, and is quite an object of curiosity to the thousands of tourists who, on board the celebrated little canal steamer *Linnet*, pass by on their way to Oban.' Glenfyne closed in 1937, although some of its buildings found new uses and survived until the 1980s, and a salmon hatchery utilised the distillery reservoir.

Scapa distillery, with Scapa Flow in the background, 1960s. Scapa dates from 1885, and was saved from fire by naval ratings billeted there in the Second World War. During the same conflict Canadian troops used Scapa's larch washbacks as baths! The spirit produced at Scapa is a principal component of Allied Distillers' popular Ballantine's blend. As a single malt Scapa has never been nearly as well known as its Orcadian neighbour, Highland Park, which is a pity, as the whisky has a rich, aromatic bouquet and a spicy, smoky flavour.

The Lomond Wash still, Scapa distillery, 1998. The Lomond still was first developed in 1954, and an example was installed at Scapa five years later. It has a short neck which gives a low level of reflux (condensing of spirit on the still neck), producing an oilier and heavier spirit than a conventional pot still.

Advertisement for Highland Park whisky, 1920s. It features the Old Man of Hoy, a landmark for travellers to Orkney by ferry from the Caithness mainland, along with a battleship. The distillery is located near Scapa Flow, one of the most famous naval bases in Britain. The Flow was the scene of the scuttling of the German High Seas Fleet after the First World War and the sinking by a German submarine of the British battleship *Royal Oak* in 1939.

Coal for Highland Park distillery being unloaded at Kirkwall pier, early 1920s. Highland Park is the northernmost distillery in Scotland and a very traditional operation, which continues to make some of its own malt using peat cut from the distillery's peat beds in the process. Contrary to popular belief heather is not burned during kilning. The whisky's characteristic heathery nose and flavour come from the Hobbister moor peat. Highland Park has been owned by Highland Distillers since 1937.

Man O' Hoy distillery yard, Stromness, Orkney, with the harbour in the background, 1924. Stromness opened in 1817, and went through the hands of six different proprietors in forty years. In 1878 it was bought by the Macpherson brothers, who ran it until the early 1900s, changing the distillery's name from Stromness to Man O' Hoy, and selling its whisky as Old Orkney. The distillery was very antiquated, and its output was only around 7,000 gallons per year. Barnard described it as 'the most remote Distillery in the Kingdom', and also bestowed on it the epithet 'quaint'.

This small, idiosyncratic pair of stills was on display in the yard of Man O' Hoy distillery in 1924, after being replaced by newer equipment. The one on the left is said to have belonged to a notorious local illicit whisky-maker before its incorporation into the distillery. Man O' Hoy fell victim to the slump of the 1920s, and closed down in 1928. Subsequently a local authority housing development filled the site, and the late Orcadian writer George Mackay Brown lived in one of its properties for many years.

Isle of Arran distillery, Lochranza, 1996. The Isle of Arran distillery is Scotland's newest, having opened in 1995. Prior to its construction the last legal whisky-making operation on Arran was at Lagg, in 1837. Arran has a long tradition of distilling, both legally and illegally, and 'Arran Water' enjoyed great popularity in Glasgow and the west of Scotland. The new distillery is traditional in design, with one pair of stills, and incorporates impressive visitor facilities. Sampling the immature make from Arran suggests that in due course this will be an island malt of distinction.

Talisker distillery and Loch Harport, with the Cuillin Hills in the background, early 1960s. Talisker dates from 1830, and Alfred Barnard observed: 'Driving along we were struck with the picturesque situation of the Distillery, which stands on the very shore of Loch Harport, one of the most beautiful sea-lochs on this side of the island.' Talisker is the most westerly distillery in Scotland, and one of UDV's Classic Malts. Triple-distillation is usually thought to be the preserve of Lowland distilleries, but the great Skye malt was at one time triple-distilled, though the practice was abandoned in 1928.

CHAPTER EIGHT

WHISKY REGIONS:
SPEYSIDE

Moving casks, The Glenlivet distillery, 1980.

Speyside came to merit a distilling category of its own during the second half of the nineteenth century, when the growth in sales of blended whisky brought a boom to the area. Speyside boasted ideal whisky-making water, an abundance of local barley and good rail links. Its complex, elegant, mellow whiskies became great favourites with the blenders. Of the thirty-three distilleries that opened in Scotland during the last decade of the nineteenth century, no fewer than twenty-one were located on Speyside. Today more than half of the country's working distilleries are in the region, and the dozen malts categorised by blenders as 'Top Class' are all Speysides.

The area of Speyside whisky production has been described as a 'golden triangle', bounded by the city of Elgin and the whisky-making towns of Rothes, Keith and Dufftown, For distilling purposes Speyside can be defined as extending from the River Findhorn in the west to the River Deveron in the east, and as far south as the latitude of Aberdeen.

Dufftown is the whisky 'capital' of Speyside, and it takes its name from James Duff, Fourth Earl of Fife, who founded the town in 1817. The River Fiddich has its confluence with the Dullan close to Dufftown, and the quality of local water sources is one of the principal reasons why Dufftown became such a major centre for distilling. Dufftown is home to one of the best-known names in the world of whisky distilling – Glenfiddich. Glenfiddich distillery is run by the family company of William Grant & Sons, who also own neighbouring Balvenie distillery. A new plant, called Kininvie, was constructed alongside Balvenie in 1990 in order to provide a third malt for the popular Grant's 'Founders Reserve' blend. Glenfiddich was only the second distillery to be built in Dufftown, with Mortlach having been founded in 1823. William Grant worked at Mortlach as book-keeper and eventually as manager before leaving to build his own rival distillery at the opposite side of town.

As the 1890s 'whisky boom' gripped Scotland, Balvenie, Convalmore, Parkmore, Dufftown and Glendullan distilleries were all built within a period of five years, and with the completion of Glendullan in 1897 the rhyme 'Rome was built on seven hills, and Dufftown stands on seven stills' was coined. Prior to the company's acquisition by DCL, Bell's built a large, modern distillery next to their Dufftown plant in 1974, naming it Pittyvaich, but that has not worked commercially since 1993, and is now used for experimental distillation by UDV. Parkmore and Convalmore are silent, so despite the construction of Kininvie by William Grant, Dufftown currently only stands on six fully-working stills.

The Glenlivet ranks alongside Glenfiddich as one of the best-known names in Scotch whisky around the world. According to Neil Gunn, 'Historically speaking, Glenlivet is a synonym for the "real stuff".' The 14 mile long glen from which the distillery takes its name is situated in the Banffshire Highlands, and it is said that as many as two hundred illicit stills were in operation in Glenlivet at the end of the eighteenth century. In addition to the natural gifts of readily obtainable barley, excellent water and peat, Glenlivet had the priceless assets of remoteness and inaccessibility.

George Smith took out a licence to distil at Upper Drumin in the glen in 1824, and such was the success of the new venture that in 1850 a larger distillery at

Delnabo, near Tomintoul, was built. That in turn was superseded by the present plant at Minmore. Not surprisingly, other distillers in the area decided to cash in on the Glenlivet name. By the 1880s so many whisky-makers throughout Strathspey were using the name Glenlivet alongside their own names on the pretext of vague stylistic or geographical similarities that it was jokingly referred to as 'the longest glen in Scotland'.

George Smith's son and successor John instigated litigation in an attempt to protect the integrity of the distillery name and its whisky, and the result was an agreement that only G. & J.G. Smith were allowed to use the definite article in front of the Glenlivet name. Other distillers could, however, use 'Glenlivet' as a hyphenated addition to their own distillery titles. At one time no fewer than twenty-eight distilleries chose to incorporate the Glenlivet suffix, but the practice has dwindled during the past couple of decades.

In 1977 The Glenlivet Distillers Ltd was acquired by Seagram, which brought not only The Glenlivet but also the Rothes distilleries of Glen Grant and Caperdonich into the Seagram fold, along with the sister distilleries of Longmorn and Benriach, near Elgin.

Seagram already owned Glen Keith and the historic Strathisla distillery in the town of Keith, and during the mid-1970s they also constructed two state-of-the-art distilleries in the shape of Braes of Glenlivet and Allt a Bhainne, in order to provide malt for their Chivas Regal, Passport, and 100 Pipers blends.

The Macallan is another Speyside malt of world stature to compare with The Glenlivet, Glenfiddich and the other leading whiskies produced in a small area of north-east Scotland. All Macallan sold as single malt is matured exclusively in sherry wood, which is an expensive policy as sherry casks cost around ten times as much as bourbon casks. The policy has been repaid, however, by a top three placing in UK single malt sales, and it gives the whisky its distinctive rich, robust, full-bodied nature, which contrasts with the lighter and drier style of many Speyside malts such as Glenfiddich.

Away from the distilling capital of Dufftown, Rothes and Keith are two other centres of whisky-making, with Glen Grant, Caperdonich, Glen Rothes, Speyburn and Glen Spey being located in and around the former, while Glen Keith, Strathmill, Strathisla and Aultmore are situated in the vicinity of the latter. The city of Elgin and its environs are home to a handful of distilleries, many of which produce notably good malts. These include Glen Moray, Linkwood, Benriach, Longmorn, Glen Elgin, Coleburn, Glenlossie, Mannochmore and Milton Duff.

The River Spey at Craigellachie. The Spey is as renowned for its fine fishing as it is for the whiskies made in its proximity. It is Scotland's second longest and fastest flowing river. The confluence of the Spey and the River Fiddich is at Craigellachie, where Thomas Telford built this cast-iron bridge in 1814.

The 'Whisky Train' entrance display made from disused casks at the Speyside Cooperage, Craigellachie. The cooperage features on the official Speyside Malt Whisky Trail, along with seven distilleries. The trail stretches for 70 miles, and all the distilleries on it offer extensive visitor facilities. They include Cardhu, Glenfarclas, Glen Grant, Glenfiddich, The Glenlivet, Strathisla and the distillery museum of Dallas Dhu.

Dufftown is famous far and near,
And many days are ' letter'd red ';
The very spot for **H**olidays,
And who comes now but good King **N**ed.

G.R.

The King visits the Capital of Malt Whisky. This visit to Dufftown by King Edward VII (1901–10), believed to have been in 1907, probably took place during one of his regular autumn stays with the Sassoon family at Tulchan Lodge near Grantown-on-Spey.

Dufftown clock tower, 1998. The tower was formerly the town gaol, and at one time an audacious site for an illicit still, close to the local excise office. Smoke travelled up a narrow chimney which appeared to be a lightning conductor, and nobody remarked on the aroma of distilling in a town so devoted to legitimate whisky-making. The story goes that the still was only detected when the clock stopped, and one of the town's excise officers who was a keen amateur clock-repairer bustled up the tower to mend it, only to be faced with a bubbling still!

The entrance to Glenfiddich distillery, 1950s. The first spirit ran from the stills on Christmas Day 1887, and Glenfiddich is now one of the most productive malt distilleries in Scotland. The number of stills may have increased, but each one is still modelled on the originals which William Grant bought second-hand from another Speyside distillery, Cardhu, when he was setting up his enterprise.

William Grant & Sons was the first company to open a purpose-built distillery visitor centre, at Glenfiddich, but public interest in whisky-making was not a new phenomenon. The photograph features a visit to the distillery in 1899, believed to have been made by members of the Banffshire Field Club.

An early portrait of William Grant (1839–1923) and his wife Elizabeth Duncan Grant (1842–1925). William Grant & Sons was the first company to see the potential for sales of single malt whisky in a market totally dominated by blends, and since the 1960s they have promoted Glenfiddich with great ability and tenacity. It is a tribute to their continued skill that in a now crowded market-place for malts, Glenfiddich remains the bestselling malt both in Britain and abroad.

William Grant and his family, reproduced from the family Bible. William Grant ran Glenfiddich with the help of three of his sons, George, Charlie and Alec. When the Supervisor of the Inland Revenue paid his first visit to the distillery, he was surprised to discover mathematical and Latin text books lying around the works. He was even more surprised when informed that they belonged to the maltman, the tun room man and the stillman. These were the three Grant boys, two of whom became doctors, although still remaining active in the business, while Charles went on to own the Glendronach distillery, near Huntly.

Parkmore distillery, Dufftown, 1998. Parkmore fell silent in 1931, having been acquired by DCL just six years previously. Because it did not suffer from the sometimes brutal upgrading and expansion projects visited on so many distilleries from the 1950s onwards, Parkmore remains externally one of the finest examples of late Victorian distillery architecture in existence. For many years after its closure Parkmore was the base of DCL's engineering 'flying squad', and its extensive warehousing capacity continues to be utilised.

Convalmore distillery, 1998. Convalmore is situated next to Balvenie distillery, and was closed down in 1985, during DCL cutbacks, having originally passed to the company in the same year as Parkmore. Seven years after its closure Convalmore was sold to William Grant & Sons, for its warehousing capacity.

Moving casks at Longmorn distillery, 1980. Longmorn dates from 1894–5, and although far from being a household name this is one of the classic malts of Speyside. The distillery and its make were originally known as Longmorn-Glenlivet, but in order to protect the cachet of *The* Glenlivet, the Chivas & Glenlivet Group has dropped the suffix, and removed the white-lettered words from the distillery roof. Independent bottlers, however, continue to label the whisky as Longmorn-Glenlivet.

Strathisla distillery, 1924. Strathisla dates from 1786, and is the oldest working distillery on Speyside. At the time this photograph was taken the distillery was known as Milltown, a name it retained until the 1950s. The bearded figure in the foreground is William Davidson, then an employee for seventy-five years!

Glenfarclas distillery workforce, *c. 1883*. Few family-owned distilleries have survived the pressures of takeovers, amalgamation and consolidation that have been such a feature of the whisky industry this century. As well as Grant's of Glenfiddich, Speyside can boast another family distillery company in the shape of Glenfarclas, owned by a separate branch of the Grant family. The managing director John Grant is the great-great grandson of John Grant, who took on the distillery in 1865, some thirty years after an initial licence was granted. Glenfarclas is located at Ballindalloch, near Aberlour, and boasts the six largest stills on Speyside.

Glen Grant workforce, 1934. Glen Grant distillery in Rothes was founded in 1840 by the brothers John and James Grant, and it was James Grant's son, also James (1847–1931), who shaped the present-day operation, expanding what was already one of the largest whisky-making plants in Scotland. Glen Grant was being bottled and sold as a single malt in Scotland early in the twentieth century, when few other distillers had even considered the possibility. Younger expressions of the whisky are now extremely popular in European markets, most notably Italy.

James Grant, or 'The Major' as he was universally known, lived the life of a Highland laird, fishing and hunting, while he also travelled widely in Africa and India. At the age of seventy-four he caught no fewer than thirty-eight salmon and grilse in a single fishing expedition. Such was the respect he commanded that when he died in 1931 four hundred mourners travelled to Elgin with the funeral train, though work at Glen Grant distillery continued on the morning of the burial, and the staff attended the service in their working clothes.

During a visit to Matabeleland in 1898 James Grant's hunting party found an abandoned child, and The Major brought him back to Rothes and educated him. Biawa Makalaga became his butler, and after Grant's death he lived on in Glen Grant House until he died in his mid-eighties in 1972.

The Glenlivet distillery, Minmore, 1988. George Smith was the first distiller to take out a licence in the wake of the 1823 Excise Act, working from a site at Upper Drumin, not far from the present Glenlivet plant. After Alfred Barnard had toured The Glenlivet distillery, he wrote: 'This neighbourhood has always been famous for its whisky. Formerly smuggling houses were scattered on every rill, all over the mountain glens, and at that time the smugglers used to lash the kegs of spirit on their backs, and take them all the way to Aberdeen or Perth for disposal.'

One of The Glenlivet's fleet of steam lorries, 1920s. Such was the reputation of Glenlivet whisky that when King George IV visited Scotland in 1822 he insisted on being supplied with illegally distilled whisky from the glen.

The former Tamdhu station, 1998. Tamdhu distillery lies close to the River Spey, between Knockando and Cardhu distilleries, and was built during the whisky-boom years of the 1890s. It was served by a branch line of the Strathspey railway, which closed in 1968, and the station buildings were subsequently converted into visitor facilities. Tamdhu belongs to Highland Distillers, and is a component of the company's Famous Grouse blend.

Knockando distillery office, 1998. Knockando is situated just a few hundred yards from Tamdhu distillery, and also dates from the 1890s. It was bought by W. & A. Gilbey in 1904 for £3,500, a price that reflected the bust which had followed boom. Gilbey had already acquired Strathmill and Glen Spey distilleries, and the firm was ultimately to become part of International Distillers & Vintners, now absorbed into UDV.

Cardhu distillery is on the Malt Whisky Trail, and has its origins in an illicit operation carried out on the site by John and Ellen Cumming, who proceeded to take out a licence in the wake of the 1823 Excise Act. For much of its existence the distillery was called Cardow, but in 1983 its owners DCL renamed it Cardhu, the Gaelic for black fort.

Delivering barley to Dailuaine distillery, Carron, near Aberlour, early 1920s. Dailuaine opened in 1851, and when Barnard visited – a few years before the distilling boom hit Dufftown – he climbed a slope near the distillery at the suggestion of the manager. He noted that he could see 'almost in a circle, no less than seven other Distilleries: The Glenlivet, Glenfarcles, Cragganmore, Cardow, Benrinnes, Aberlour and Macallan, forming most of the celebrated Speyside Distilleries, Glen Rothes, Glen Spey, Glen Grant and Mortlach being hidden from our view by hills and woods'. Dailuaine is one of fourteen Speyside plants operated by UDV.

The stillhouse, Dallas Dhu, Forres, early 1920s. The interiors of very few distilleries survive in anything like their inter-war form, but Dallas Dhu is an exception, having escaped major upgrading and redevelopment. This was largely because the distillery's water supply was unable to cope with extra demands. Its modest capacity and lack of modernity made Dallas Dhu an obvious candidate for closure by DCL during the early 1980s, but these factors also mean that the preserved distillery allows visitors to experience the way distilling was carried out a generation and more ago.

A memorandum of August 1898 from William Teacher & Sons Ltd to James Innes of Huntly, regarding payments made in relation to the construction of Ardmore distillery, which opened that year. Ardmore was designed by Charles Doig for the Glasgow-based Teacher's company, and was located on the eastern fringes of Speyside, at Kennethmont in Aberdeenshire.

The terms of engagement for staff at Ardmore, 1898, from the distillery's first wages book. John Watt was appointed Head Maltman, at a wage of 23s per week, along with 'Free house, and coals at the same rate as they cost the distiller'. The name of Teacher's principal blended whisky, Highland Cream, had been registered in 1884, and Ardmore was constructed in order to provide malt for the firm's expanding blended whisky business. Ardmore remains a principal contributor to Highland Cream. William Teacher & Sons Ltd is now owned by Allied Distillers.

A 1927 bottling of sixteen-year-old Parkmore single malt.

A bottle of Glendronach 'Self Whisky', *c.* 1930. The expression self whisky predates the now more usual single malt. The declaration 'Most suitable for medicinal purposes' is a throwback to the early sixteenth century when the Guild of Barber Surgeons had a monopoly on whisky-making in Edinburgh. The Glendronach distillery lies 5 miles north-east of Huntly, and dates from 1826. William Grant's son, Charles, purchased the distillery in 1920, and sold it to William Teacher & Sons forty years later. Like Ardmore it is a major component of the Teacher's Highland Cream blend.

A rare cask sample of nineteenth-century Macallan. The Macallan is now part of Highland Distillers' portfolio of high-quality distilleries, and rare and vintage examples of the whisky invariably make high prices at auction. This example, distilled in 1872, was top lot at Christie's Scotland April 1998 whisky sale, when it fetched no less than £5,520.

CHAPTER NINE

WHISKY REGIONS: CAMPBELTOWN

Scotia distillery buildings, including the mash house, early 1920s.

As Speyside malts increased in popularity with blenders, so the fortunes of the Campbeltown region waned during the late nineteenth and early twentieth centuries. It is fascinating to explore the rise and fall of Campbeltown as a distilling centre, to consider why one isolated fishing port at the southern end of the long Kintyre peninsula in Argyllshire should have been able to boast no fewer than thirty-four distilleries at different times during little more than a century of its history.

As the crow flies, Campbeltown is slightly closer to the Bushmills distillery on the Northern Irish coast of Antrim than it is to the nearest Islay distilleries of Ardbeg, Lagavulin and Laphroaig, and the art of distilling may have arrived in Scotland by way of Kintyre from the north of Ireland.

The earliest written reference to whisky-making in the area dates from 1591, and long before large-scale legal distilling became a feature of Campbeltown the area was a noted centre for illicit production. This was partly owing to its isolated nature, the availability of local barley and peat, and even coal from the Drumlemble mine near Campbeltown. The port also boasts a fine natural harbour. The peaty illegal make of the Campbeltown stills became far more popular in Glasgow and its neighbouring towns than Lowland whisky.

Writing in 1772, Thomas Pennant noted disapprovingly: 'Notwithstanding the quantity of bear [a kind of barley] raised, there is often a sort of dearth, the inhabitants being mad enough to convert their bread into poison, distilling annually six thousand bolls of grain into whisky.' According to the *Old Statistical Account*, in 1795 there were thirty-two licensed stills in and around Campbeltown, annually producing in excess of 26,000 gallons of whisky. The *Account* noted: 'Next to the fishing of herring, the business most attended to in Campbeltown is the distilling of whisky. . . .' In August 1873 no fewer than 29,000 gallons of whisky were produced in Campbeltown in *one week*.

The 1823 Excise Act led to an expansion of legal distilling activities in Kintyre, as it did throughout Scotland, and by 1837 twenty-eight distilleries had been established in Campbeltown. There was a ready market for their make in the expanding city of Glasgow and the rest of the industrial west of Scotland, which was easily accessible by sea, if less so by road. When Alfred Barnard visited Campbeltown half a century later he toured twenty-one distilleries, and called Campbeltown 'The Whisky City'. In 1885 total output for the Campbeltown distilleries was 1,938,000 gallons, and more than 250 men were directly employed in distilling.

By 1925, however, only twelve Campbeltown distilleries were working, and in 1934 just Rieclachan, Glen Scotia and Springbank remained. Rieclachan closed in that year, and Glen Scotia is now mothballed. Fortunately Springbank is one of the world's great whiskies, and as a family-owned firm with a strong demand for its product, the future for this last survivor of a fascinating distilling tradition looks bright. Springbank has the characteristic saltiness associated with the Campbeltown style, which is not too far removed from some of the less assertive Islay malts. Along with Glenfiddich, it is the only malt whisky still bottled at source.

When the Campbeltown distilleries were at their most productive local farmers could not meet the demand for barley, and large quantities were imported by sea from other parts of Scotland and abroad, most notably from the Baltic ports. Campbeltown distillers ran a grain-drying co-operative from the early 1890s, with wet draff being sold locally, while the dried grains were exported as feedstuff for the horses of the German army.

The town was, in part, a victim of its own success, as some of the less scrupulous distilleries began to turn out inferior spirit in order to satisfy the voracious appetites of the blenders and undercut their competitors around the turn of the century. The period of Prohibition in the USA, from 1919 to 1933, also gave the less fastidious Campbeltown distillers the opportunity to make a quick profit by providing 'bootleg hootch' for the speakeasies of New York, Chicago and other American cities. 'Stinking fish' was just one pejorative description of the town's produce, and the commentator was not talking about the fruits of the valuable herring trade.

By the 1920s Campbeltown whiskies had such a poor reputation that the proprietors of Hazelburn, the largest distillery in town, wrote to customers advising them that it was no longer making Campbeltown whisky, but was now producing Kintyre whisky. The ploy was unsuccessful, however, and Hazelburn closed in 1925, having been taken over by Mackie & Co. in 1920, and subsequently absorbed into the DCL empire.

The onset of prohibition in the USA from 1919 was a major blow to the Campbeltown distillers, who had extensive trade with North America, and an additional difficulty for them was the closure of Drumlemble colliery in 1923, which brought to an end the supply of comparatively cheap fuel. Extremely poor road links to Glasgow and other important markets were also beginning to take their toll by the 1920s.

The backstreets of Campbeltown still contain many traces of the town's distilling heritage, usually in the form of derelict warehouses and converted buildings, and the visitor cannot fail to notice that Campbeltown is very well supplied with churches, many of them constructed on a comparatively grand scale. They are a legacy of the heyday of distilling, when local entrepreneurs who had prospered in the industry attempted to ensure their access to Heaven by endowing places of worship, fearing that their riches had been acquired in a morally questionable manner. After spending time in Kintyre during the summer of 1886, Barnard noted: 'it is said that there are nearly as many places of worship as distilleries in the town'.

Many commentators now dismiss Campbeltown as a whisky region, on the grounds that only one distillery remains in production, but for its historic contribution to distilling history alone Campbeltown surely deserves to retain its status as one of Scotland's designated areas for malt whisky-making.

Springbank distillery office, early 1920s. The distillery dates from 1828, and was the fourteenth of the thirty-four licensed distilleries documented as being built in Campbeltown. It stands on Longrow, where it now incorporates parts of five other Campbeltown distilleries, namely Rieclachan, Springside, Union, Argyll and Longrow.

Springbank distillery entrance, 1991. Springbank is still in the hands of its founding family, the Mitchells, and the distillery produces two different malt whiskies from one set of stills. There are two wash stills and one spirit still, and the standard Springbank is effectively distilled two and a half times. A more heavily peated malt whisky, called Longrow, is also produced in the distillery from time to time.

Scotia distillery buildings, including the mash house, early 1920s. The distillery dates from 1832, and is now known as Glen Scotia. It is reputed to be haunted by the ghost of a former proprietor who drowned himself in Campbeltown Loch after being cheated out of £40,000 in a business venture. Traditionally the stills at Glen Scotia were left unpolished to keep them cooler, and the proximity of the Gulf Stream means that maintaining a supply of cold water for distilling has frequently been a problem.

Glen Scotia distillery, 1991. Despite upgrading and modernisation in the early 1980s – which took its capacity from two stills to ten – Glen Scotia has operated only briefly during the past two decades. Despite appearances to the contrary, the distillery was in production when this photograph was taken. It is currently owned by the Loch Lomond Distillery Co. Ltd, and though silent, there are hopes that whisky will again flow from the Scotia stills in the future.

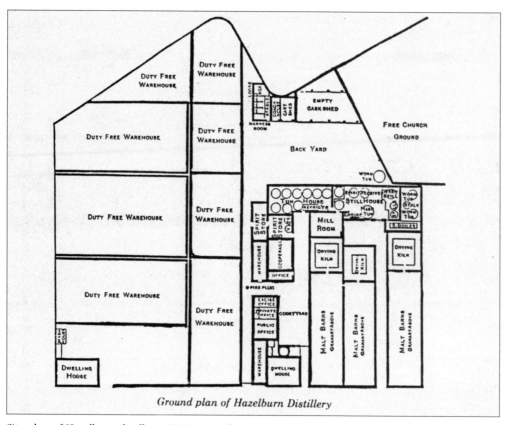

Ground plan of Hazelburn Distillery

Site plan of Hazelburn distillery, 1880s. Hazelburn distilled for exactly a century before succumbing to market forces in 1925, becoming Campbeltown's largest and most successful distillery along the way. It moved sites in 1840 from Longrow on to Millknowe Street, and boasted the town's biggest wash still, with a capacity of 7,000 gallons. The distillery had the ability to produce a quarter of a million gallons of whisky per year, and its warehouses could hold twice as much maturing spirit.

Hazelburn distillery, early 1920s. Long after Hazelburn had ceased to distil, DCL used the warehousing to mature whisky made in its Islay distilleries. Casks of spirit were taken the short trip from Port Ellen to Campbeltown by boat, where maritime conditions replicated those on Islay. This saved constructing additional warehousing on the island. The Hazelburn site has now become a business park, incorporating some of the original buildings.

Benmore distillery courtyard, early 1920s. Benmore was built in Saddell Street in 1868 by Glasgow-based Bulloch Lade & Co., and in 1929 it came under the ownership of DCL, though distilling had ceased two years earlier.

Benmore distillery, 1991. Structurally Benmore has survived better than most defunct Campbeltown distilleries. After closure the Benmore site was subsequently sold to West Coast Motor Services, and it has remained a bus depot ever since. The pagoda roof may have gone from the former maltings, but Benmore was the first Campbeltown distillery to boast such a feature.

Lochhead distillery, early 1920s. Lochhead was founded in 1824, and from 1895 until 1920 it was owned by J.B. Sheriff and Co. Ltd, who expanded it at the turn of the century, though the operation already boasted the borough's biggest mash tun. Sheriff also had interests in Lochindaal and Bowmore distilleries on Islay, but when the company collapsed in 1920 Benmore Distilleries Ltd acquired Lochhead, which ultimately passed to DCL in 1929, a year after distilling had ceased. Much of Lochhead remained intact until the 1990s, when the site was cleared for a supermarket development.

Albyn was one of Campbeltown's smaller distilleries, producing around 85,000 gallons of spirit per year when operating at full stretch. It was built in 1830 by the McKersie family, who also bought Lochruan distillery in the 1860s. Albyn was silent during the First World War, but re-opened in its aftermath, only to close again in 1920. In 1928 it was sold and the site redeveloped. This photograph from soon after the First World War features Donald McCallum (right), who at the time was the oldest distillery employee in Campbeltown, having served at Albyn for forty-eight years.

Kinloch distillery, wash, feints and spirit pumps, early 1920s. Kinloch was one of Campbeltown's earlier distilleries, starting production in 1823 on the site of a former maltings. Alfred Barnard wrote of Kinloch: 'It is quite close to the loch and harbour, and the continual movement on the water of fishing boats and steamers, together with the bustle and traffic on the wharf, gives this Distillery more life and animation than any of the others.' Kinloch ceased production in 1926, and its owner David MacCallum subsequently gave the distillery to the local authority as a site for housing development.

Glenside distillery yard and offices, early 1920s. Glenside was built in 1834, and Barnard noted in 1886 that it consisted of 'an irregular section of buildings, which are all enclosed and entered by an arched gateway. During the last three years many improvements have been made, but nothing short of pulling the place down, and rebuilding it, could ever give it the appearance of a modern Distillery, and, as the manager remarked, any such alterations would not improve the Whisky or increase the sale.' Glenside closed in 1926, when it remained as old-fashioned as at the time of Barnard's visit.

Campbeltown Creamery Ltd, Witchburn Road, 1991. Situated half a mile from the town centre, the site now occupied by this operation was formerly home to Burnside distillery, which existed between 1825 and the early 1920s. When the distillery closed the premises were converted into a creamery, and the old buildings still stand at the heart of the expanded plant.

Removing 2,200 casks of Craigellachie whisky to Campbeltown, early 1920s. The Craigellachie distillery on Speyside was owned by Mackie & Co. Ltd, and in 1920 the company also acquired Hazelburn distillery. This large consignment of Craigellachie whisky was presumably being shipped to Campbeltown to take advantage of Hazelburn's warehousing capacity.

CHAPTER TEN

WHISKY REGIONS:
ISLAY

Lochindaal distillery, 1922.

Islay is the largest and most southerly of the Inner Hebridean islands, and is as much a place of pilgrimage for devotees of malt whisky as Speyside, though from a stylistic point of view the two regions could not produce more different whiskies. Islays are the most assertive and distinctive malts in existence. Strung out along the southern shore of the island, to the east of Port Ellen, in the area known as Kildalton, is the famous trinity of Laphroaig, Lagavulin and Ardbeg. These are the most strongly flavoured, heavily peaty and pungent whiskies made in Scotland. Islays also tend to embrace an iodine-like, seaweedy character, which is notable in the oily, northern malt of Caol Ila. Nearby Bunnahabhain distillery turns out one of the lightest Islays, along with Bruichladdich to the west, which features tall stills and light peating.

The characteristics of Islay whiskies owe much to the vast areas of peat, which are such a distinctive feature of the landscape, and to the maritime location. The peat takes a seaweed aroma from the sea breezes and also contains sea vegetation. This briny characteristic is passed on to the water which flows through it, and is subsequently used to steep the barley in the island's three maltings, at Bowmore, Laphroaig and Port Ellen. The peaty water is also used during the mashing process. The vast, modern maltings located next to the silent Port Ellen distillery provide malt for all the island's distilleries, as even those that retain their own floor maltings need to buy in extra stocks to meet their distilling requirements. Each distillery specifies its own level of peating, and Ardbeg, Laphroaig and Lagavulin have the highest peat specification. Sea air penetrates the casks of spirit during maturation, adding to the characteristic nose and flavour.

From at least the late eighteenth century whiskies produced on Islay have been noted for their individuality of flavour, and Thomas Pennant observed after visiting Islay in 1772 that 'in old times the distillation was from thyme, mint, anise, and other fragrant herbs'. The remote Oa peninsula in the south-west of Islay was a centre for illegal distillation, and there were also a number of inland, farm-based distilleries on the island. Remains of four such operations can be seen at Tallant Farm by Bowmore, at Newton and Lossit, Bridgend, and at Octomore Farm above Port Charlotte.

When Barnard spent time on Islay in 1886, he noted that 'ten years ago there were but few distilleries in Islay, but the increasing demand for this valuable make of Whisky for blending purposes, encouraged further enterprise in the extension of existing Distilleries and the erection of new ones'. Bruichladdich had opened five years prior to Barnard's visit, while the last distillery to be built on Islay was Bunnahabhain, near Port Askaig, which was constructed around the same time.

Twenty-three distilleries have been licensed on Islay since the mid-eighteenth century, and compared to the decimation of the Campbeltown whisky industry, just a few miles to the east, Islay has managed to defy most periods of decline. Perhaps the secret of Islay's enduring success as a whisky-making region lies in the fact that the island's malts are essential, albeit in small quantities, to any self-respecting blended whisky. Unlike the whiskies of nearby Campbeltown they have also retained a reputation for excellence through the years, gaining a devoted following of single malt drinkers along the way.

There are currently six working distilleries on the island, the oldest of which is Bowmore, and this century only Lochindaal distillery at Port Charlotte has been totally lost, closing in the 1920s. Port Ellen distillery became a victim of DCL's 1983 round of closures but remains largely intact, while Bruichladdich fell silent in 1995, though it is intended to distil there on an occasional basis in the future. The shutdown of Bruichladdich leaves Talisker on Skye as the most westerly distillery in production. Heading west from Bruichladdich, the next distillery is to be found in Nova Scotia.

Positive news for the Islay distilling industry is that after enduring many years of intermittent production, the future of Ardbeg appears to be secure. The distillery was acquired by Glenmorangie Plc in 1997 from Laphroaig's owner Allied Distillers, and Glenmorangie have invested heavily in the plant itself, a visitor centre and in promotion of the malt. For many connoisseurs Ardbeg is *the* regional classic.

When Barnard visited Islay Caol Ila had not long been expanded, and he wrote: 'The buildings connected with the works are of solid construction and handsome appearance; they are all built of stone, hewn from the adjacent rocks.' Sadly Caol Ila no longer presents such a handsome appearance, having been rebuilt in 1973 in the factory-like style favoured by DCL at the time. Production capacity was trebled, and Caol Ila is now one of the largest distilleries in the Hebrides. The view from the stillhouse across the Sound of Islay to the neighbouring island of Jura is breathtaking. Barnard's remark that 'Caol Ila Distillery stands in the wildest and most picturesque locality we have seen' still holds true today. The distillery dates from 1846, and passed to DCL in 1927. Once Caol Ila had been expanded in the 1970s the position of the company's Port Ellen distillery was always perilous, as both malts were no longer needed for blending purposes. Caol Isla became DCL's main Islay blending malt, while Lagavulin is its flagship Islay single.

Cutting peat, Islay, 1990s. Peat covers around 25 per cent of the surface area of Islay, in some places up to a depth of 100 ft. Alfred Barnard wrote that 'the Distillers maintain that the sea air has no effect whatever on the Whisky, and that the peculiarity of the Islay make arises principally from the flavour of the peat, dug on the island, which is more strongly impregnated with moss than some other districts'.

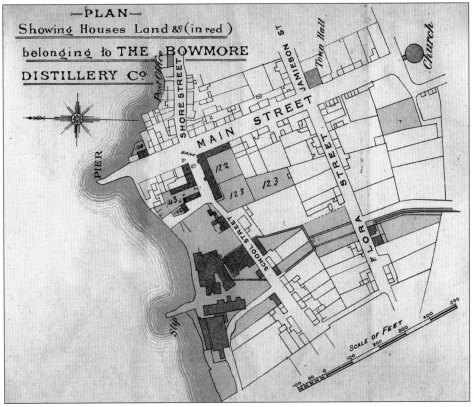

Plan of Bowmore, early twentieth century, featuring the site of Bowmore distillery. The distillery had been founded in 1779, and was in the ownership of the Bowmore Distillery Co. from 1892 until 1925. Bowmore has remained very traditional in its production practices, having its own peat bog and retaining a malting floor which provides the plant with around one-third of its malt requirements.

Bowmore distillery from Loch Indaal, 1990s. At high tide the seawater rises several feet up the side of the warehouse. In 1963 the Glasgow-based whisky broking firm of Stanley P. Morrison Ltd purchased Bowmore distillery, and it remained in their ownership until the company – now known as Morrison Bowmore Distillers Ltd – was absorbed by Suntory in 1994. Bowmore single malt has long enjoyed an enthusiastic following in Japan.

Bruichladdich distillery, 1991. Bruichladdich began production on the western shore of Loch Indaal in 1881, and was one of the first distilleries to be constructed from an innovative new building material called concrete. In 1968 Bruichladdich was bought by Invergordon Distillers, who extended it in 1975, raising production capacity to 800,000 proof gallons per year. The distillery is now owned by JBB (Greater Europe) Plc.

Lochindaal distillery, 1922. Lochindaal was located in the village of Port Charlotte, 2 miles beyond Bruichladdich, and was built in 1829. Barnard observed that Port Charlotte was 'a village of little importance and interest except for the large Distillery owned by Mr Sheriff, which employs a number of the labouring class, and gives some little life to the locality'.

Lochindaal distillery yard, 1922, a year after the distillery had been sold by the Sheriff family to Benmore Distilleries Ltd, whose name is stencilled on to the casks shown in the photograph. After Benmore was acquired by DCL in 1929 the distillery was immediately closed. The malt barns were subsequently incorporated into the Islay Creamery, while some warehousing continued to be used to mature whisky from other distilleries for many years.

Port Ellen distillery, 1904. Port Ellen distillery opened for business in 1825, and has an important place in the history of Scotch whisky. The spirit safe was developed there, and it was also at Port Ellen that Aeneas Coffey and Robert Stein conducted pioneering work on the patent still. The first direct export of whisky to the USA took place from Port Ellen distillery when it was owned by whisky magnate John Ramsay.

Port Ellen distillery and maltings, 1991. Despite extensive modernisation in 1967 Port Ellen distillery was one of the DCL plants to close in 1983, and there seems little chance that whisky will ever be made there again. Some of the distilling plant from Port Ellen has found a new lease of life in India and Russia. The massive malting complex of 1973 dwarfs the distillery; it is capable of producing 400 tonnes of malted barley per week.

Laphroaig distillery and bay, late nineteenth century. Coal was brought into Laphroaig bay in rowing boats from puffers anchored in deeper water, and horse-drawn distillery carts went out to meet the boats in the shallows, where the cargo was transferred. In 1886 Alfred Barnard described Laphroaig as 'a thick and pungent spirit of a peculiar "peat reek" flavour', and though today's Laphroaig is less intense than its predecessors, it remains one of the world's most characterful whiskies.

Bessie Williamson working at the Laphroaig spirit safe, late 1950s. Laphroaig was established in 1815 by Alex and Donald Johnston, and the latter brother suffered the misfortune of dying in 1847 as a result of falling into a vat of pot ale. Laphroaig remained in the Johnston family until 1954, when, on the death of Ian Hunter, the distillery was bequeathed to Bessie Williamson, Hunter's company secretary. Bessie Williamson was one of very few women to have run a distillery, but was highly respected within the industry.

Floating a new boiler for Laphroaig to the distillery from Port Ellen jetty, 1906. Laphroaig has the distinction of being the only Islay malt to figure in the 'top ten' of world malt whisky sales. Part of the Laphroaig site was formerly the Ardenistle distillery, which was operated between 1837 and 1842 by James and Andrew Stein. Laphroaig is now owned by Allied Distillers Ltd.

Workmen on the pier at Lagavulin distillery, July 1912. All the surviving Islay distilleries are located beside the sea, and in 1924 DCL, owners of Lagavulin and Caol Ila on Islay, purchased a 'puffer', or coaster, named the *Pibroch*. This vessel served the company's Islay distilleries, and also Talisker on Skye, and was a familiar sight around the Hebrides for many years. The introduction of roll on/roll off ferries to Islay in 1974 brought to an end individual distillery deliveries by sea. In 1999 the Lagavulin pier was reconstructed as part of a £1.75m refurbishment project.

Lagavulin distillery, *c.* 1904, with a vessel discharging its cargo at the pier. Lagavulin traces its origins back to the 1740s, when no fewer than ten illicit stills were working close to Lagavulin Bay. Peter Mackie took over the distillery in 1889, and soon afterwards launched the White Horse blend. Lagavulin subsequently passed to DCL, and its whisky remains an important constituent of White Horse. As a single malt it is the best seller in UDV's range of Classic Malts.

Early twentieth-century bottling of Mackie's Special Reserve, distilled in the late nineteenth century. The whisky has remained clear during maturation as it was stored in what the label describes as plain wood', rather than casks that had previously contained sherry.

Stills of the Malt Mill distillery, early 1920s. The Malt Mill distillery originally opened in 1816 close to Lagavulin, and was reinstated in 1908 by Peter Mackie. Mackie's purpose in recreating Malt Mill was to produce a whisky to rival Laphroaig, with whom he was in dispute over water rights. It was set up on very traditional lines, using only peat in the kilns, but in 1962 Malt Mill was dismantled, though its coal-fired stills were given another seven years of life within the main Lagavulin stillhouse, before being replaced. The Malt Mill is now Lagavulin's reception centre.

A corner of the recently established distillery visitor centre, Ardbeg, 1998. Ardbeg is the second oldest surviving distillery on Islay, having been founded in 1815. It is fortunate to have survived at all, having experienced several prolonged periods of silence in recent years. Ardbeg was always destined to remain in the shadow of Laphroaig while Allied Distillers owned both operations, but the distillery and its single malt are now gaining a higher public profile.

Ardbeg distillery from the sea, 1998. As a whisky, Ardbeg has a reputation as an archetypal Islay, full-bodied, smoky, and with an obvious maritime influence. Traditionally, Ardbeg used the most heavily peated malt in Scotland, operating its own floor maltings until the early 1980s. Lack of fans in the malting house pagodas meant that instead of being drawn upwards quite rapidly, the peat smoke permeated very thoroughly through the malt, producing a distinctive pungency in the finished whisky.

Bunnahabhain distillery, *c.* 1904. Alfred Barnard noted: 'The Bunnahabhain Distillery was built in the year 1881, and is situated on the bay of that name. At that time this portion of the island was bare, and uninhabited, but the prosecution of the distilling industry has transformed it into a life-like and civilized colony. The works have a frontage towards the bay, and command a fine view of the opposite shore, and the celebrated "Paps of Jura". The Distillery proper is a fine pile of buildings in the form of a square, and quite enclosed.'

Bunnahabhain distillery, 1991. Today Bunnahabhain – Gaelic for mouth of the river – belongs to Highland Distillers, and the distillery community remains. Since the 1970s Bunnahabhain has been bottled as a single malt by its proprietors, and the twelve year old – quite light in character for an Islay – is particularly popular in France and the USA.

Caol Ila distillery, 1991. Alfred Barnard would not have recognised the distillery that he visited in 1886, though the approach to the plant remains dramatic. Barnard wrote that 'the way is so steep, and our nerves none of the best, that we insist upon doing the remainder of the descent on foot, much to the disgust of the driver, who muttered strange words in Gaelic'.

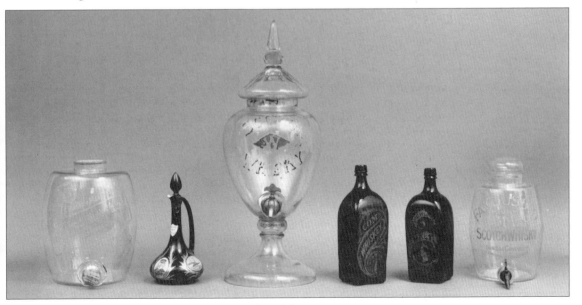

A display of nineteenth-century glass whisky vessels and dispensers.

ACKNOWLEDGEMENTS

I am indebted to a great many people for their interest, enthusiasm and unselfishness in sharing knowledge and material with me during the compilation of this book. My thanks go to all the individuals and all the companies within the whisky industry who have been associated with the project, along with the personnel of numerous Scottish libraries and archives, as well as to the staff of Sutton Publishing Ltd, particularly Simon Fletcher and Annabel Fearnley.

Especial thanks are due to Mairi Adam, Bill Bennett, Neil Boyd, Irvine Butterfield, John Campbell, Patricia Clarke, Alicia Columbine, Harold Currie, Caroline Dunbar, George Gainsburgh, Jean Gillies, Martin Green, Malcolm Greenwood, Peter Grigor, Philippa Ireland, Bill Jones, Richard Joynson, Tommy Leigh, John McDougall, John Mackie, Charles MacLean, John Marshall, Dianne O'Connor, Richard Paterson, Susan Payne, Margo Perrons, Iain Russell, Christine Thomson, Joy Thomson, Graeme Wilson, Neil Wilson.

Photographs are reproduced by kind permission of the following:

Allied Distillers Ltd (2 Glasgow Road, Dumbarton, G81 1ND): pp. 43 (lower), 53 (upper), 78 (lower), 107 (lower), 112, 131, 150, 151 (upper); Bernard Photo-Productions/JBB (Greater Europe) Plc (Dalmore House, 310 St Vincent Street, Glasgow, G2 5RG): pp. 18 (upper), 22 (lower), 37 (upper), 46 (upper), 47 (lower), 60 (upper), 77 (upper), 102 (lower), 103 (lower), 104, 105, 106, 107 (upper), 108 (upper), 110 (upper), 111 (lower), 113 (lower), 114, 115, 130, 136 (upper), 137 (upper), 138 (lower), 139 (upper), 140, 141, 142 (lower), 148, 152 (lower); Irvine Butterfield: pp. 16, 25 (lower), 39 (lower), 90 (upper), 103 (upper), 116 (lower); Chivas & Glenlivet Group (The Ark, 201 Talgarth Road, London, W6 8BN): pp. 7, 22 (upper), 28 (upper), 29 (upper), 32 (lower), 37 (lower), 42, 52 (upper), 54, 59 (upper), 61 (lower), 63 (upper), 68 (lower), 69 (upper), 70, 71 (upper), 82, 86 (lower), 125, 126 (lower), 127, 128; Christie's Scotland Ltd (164–6 Bath Street, Glasgow, G2 4TB): pp. 22, 27, 38, 132, 152, 155 (lower); John Dewar & Sons Ltd (1700 London Road, Glasgow, G32 8XR): pp. 6, 24, 25 (upper), 29 (lower), 44 (lower), 53 (lower), 56, 57 (lower), 58, 59 (lower), 60 (upper), 69 (lower), 85, 86 (upper), 101 (upper); Jean Gillies: p. 151 (lower); Glenmorangie plc (18 Westerton Road, Broxburn, EH52 5AQ): p. 153; Glenturret Distillery Ltd (The Hosh, Crieff, Perthshire, PH7 4HA): pp. 9, 17 (upper), 99; Grant, J. & G., (Glenfarclas Distillery, Ballindalloch, AB37 9BD): pp. 61 (upper), 126 (upper); William Grant & Sons (Independence House, 84 Lower Mortlake Road, Richmond, Surrey, TW9 2HS): pp. 2, 4, 28 (lower), 36 (lower), 39 (upper), 43 (upper), 44 (upper), 45, 52 (lower), 55, 62 (upper), 63 (lower), 64, 65 (upper), 72, 79, 83, 84, 121 (upper), 122, 123; Highland Distillers plc (West Kinfauns, Perth, PH2 7ZX): p. 113 (upper); Isle of Arran Distillers Ltd (Lochranza, Isle of Arran KA27 8HJ): p. 116 (upper); Bill Jones: p. 77 (lower); Margaret Kirkby: pp. 136 (lower), 137 (lower), 139 (lower), 142 (upper), 147 (lower), 149 (lower), 154 (lower), 155 (upper); Loch Fyne Whiskies (Inveraray, Argyll PA32 8UD): pp. 48, 61 (upper); John Marshall: p. 94; Moray Council, Local Heritage Centre: p. 31; Morrison Bowmore Distillers Ltd (Springburn Road, Carlisle Street, Glasgow, G21 1EQ): pp. 47 (middle), 71 (lower), 91, 146 (upper), 147 (upper); Museum of Islay Life (Port Charlotte, Isle of Islay, PA48 7UA): pp. 64 (lower), 149 (upper), 152 (upper), 154 (upper); North British Distillery Ltd (Wheatfield Road, Edinburgh, EH11 2PX): pp. 76, 80, 81; Scotch Whisky Heritage Centre Ltd (354 Castlehill, Edinburgh, EH1 2NE): p. 48; Speyside Cooperage Ltd, Dufftown Road, Craigellachie, Banffshire, AB38 9RS): pp. 66, 67, 68 (upper); Christine Thomson: p. 100; United Distillers and Vintners Archive, pp. 78 (upper), 90 (lower), 93 (lower), 111 (upper); Ann Williams: p. 48.

INDEX

(Distilleries and brand names in *italics*)

Abbeyhill 89
Aberfeldy 25, 29, 56, 57, 58, 59, 60, 69, 84, 101
Adelphi 89
Albyn 140
Allied Distillers Ltd 74, 78, 89, 112, 145, 151, 153
Allt a Bhainne 42, 119
Annandale 88
Ardbeg 134, 144, 145, 153
Ardmore 53, 131, 132
Arran, Isle of, 97, 116
Auchentoshan 89, 91
Auchroisk 35
Auchtermuchty 94
Aultmore 46, 119

Bacardi-Martini 101
Balblair 97
Ballantines 78, 89, 112
Balvenie 43, 50, 55, 64, 65, 118, 124
Banff 37, 47, 96, 97, 104, 111
Barnard, Alfred 74, 77, 88, 89, 90, 94, 100, 108, 111, 116, 128, 130, 134, 135, 141, 144, 145, 146, 148, 150, 154, 155
Bell, Arthur & Sons Ltd 35, 93, 98, 104, 118
Benmore 139, 148
Ben Morvern 97, 109
Ben Nevis 97, 111
Benriach 54, 119
Benrinnes 44
Ben Wyvis 97, 105
Black & White 26
Bladnoch 79, 89, 93

Blair Athol 98
Bowmore 144, 145, 146
Bowmore 47, 50, 71, 140, 146, 147
Braes of Glenlivet 42, 119
Braeval 42
Bronfman, Samuel 75
Bruichladdich 144, 145, 147
Buchanan Blend 26
Buchanan, James & Co. Ltd 26, 27
Bunnahabhain 144, 154
Burns, Robert 5, 88
Burnside 142
Butterfield, Irvine 16

Cadenhead, William 7
Caledonian 22, 74, 76, 77
Cambus 36, 74, 78
Cameronbridge 74, 78
Camlachie 89, 93
Campbeltown 7, 18, 28, 134, 135, 136, 138, 139, 140, 142, 144
Canonmills 89
Caol Ila 144, 145, 151, 155
Caperdonich 119
Cardhu 120, 122, 129
Carsebridge 74
Charles, HRH Prince 43
Chivas & Glenlivet Group 40, 125
Chivas Brothers Ltd 82, 86
Chivas Regal 119
Christie's Scotland Ltd 10, 132
Clydesdale 90
Clynelish 97, 109
Coffey, Aenas 149
Coleburn 119

Convalmore 118, 124
Craigellachie 142

Dailuaine 29, 31, 130
Dallas Dhu 30, 37, 120, 130
Dalmore 97, 107
Dalwhinnie 37, 96, 101, 102
Dean 89
Dewar, John 21, 24
Dewar, John & Sons Ltd 21, 25, 27, 85, 101, 106
Dewar, Tommy 21, 24, 26, 36
Dewar's White Label 85
Diageo 35
Distillers Company Ltd (DCL) 30, 35, 36, 46, 47, 74, 76, 77, 78, 90, 96, 97, 102, 106, 109, 111, 124, 129, 130, 138, 139, 140, 145, 148, 149, 151, 152
Doig, Charles 21, 30, 31, 34, 103, 131
Dufftown 8, 42, 52, 63, 118, 119, 121, 124
Dufftown 98
Dumbarton 35, 70, 74, 78
Dundashill 89

Edinburgh 9, 20, 29, 89, 90
Edràdour 98
Elgin 29, 52, 118, 119

Fairlie, James 99
Famous Grouse, The 38, 129
Ferintosh 97, 105
Fettercairn 97
Four Crown 32

Gerston 97
Gilbey, W. & A. 129
Girvan 75, 79
Glasgow 89, 134, 135
Glen Albyn 96, 103
Glen Cawdor 96, 103
Glen Deveron 97
Glen Elgin 21, 119
Glen Garioch 96

Glen Grant 28, 29, 40, 61, 62, 119, 120, 126, 127
Glen Keith 40, 119
Glen Mhor 96, 103
Glen Moray 119
Glen Ord 106
Glen Scotia 134, 137
Glen Spey 119, 129
Glenallachie 35
Glenburgie 35
Glencadam 97
Glendronach 123, 132
Glendullan 118
Glenesk 97
Glenfarclas 16, 61, 120, 126
Glenfiddich 8, 43, 44, 45, 52, 62, 65, 68, 72, 118, 119, 120, 122, 123
Glenfyne 111
Glengoyne 96
Glenkinchie 88, 89, 90
Glenlivet 22, 38, 70, 119
Glenlivet, The 40, 59, 71, 118, 119, 120, 125, 128
Glenlochy 111
Glenlossie 30, 119
Glenmorangie 97, 108, 145
Glenrothes 119
Glen Sciennes 89
Glenside 141
Glenskiach 106
Glenturret 8, 62, 65, 99
Glenury Royal 97
Gloag, Matthew & Sons 38
Gordon & MacPhail Ltd 7
Gordon, Charles 36
Gordon, Duke of 20
Grand Metropolitan Group 35
Grandtully 100
Grange 90
Grant, J. & G. 126
Grant, Major James 126, 127
Grant, William 28, 36, 55, 63, 64, 118, 122, 123, 132

Grant, William & Sons Ltd 8, 39, 45, 52, 64, 75, 83, 84, 118, 122, 123, 124
Guinness & Sons, Arthur Ltd 35
Gunn, Neil 7, 9, 10, 103, 110, 118

Haig, John 13, 74
Haig, John & Co. Ltd 27, 103
Hakushu 47
Hazelburn 135, 138, 142
Highland Distillers Co. Plc 99, 113, 129, 132, 154
Highland Park 30, 50, 88, 97, 112, 113
Hill Thomson & Co. 37
Hiram Walker 35, 70, 78, 110
Hobbs, Joseph 111
Hunter, Ian 150

Inchgower 96, 104
International Distillers & Vintners Group (IDV) 129
Inver House Distillers Ltd 110
Inveralmond 44, 85, 86
Invergordon 75, 107
Invergordon Distillers 147
Inverleven 89
Inverness 96, 97, 103, 104

Jim Beam Brands (Greater Europe) Plc (JBB) 75, 107, 147
Johnnie Walker 27
Johnston, D. & Co. Ltd 150
Jura, Isle of 97

Keith 29, 40, 46, 70, 118, 119
Kilbagie 88
Kinclaith 89
Kininvie 118
Kinloch 141
Knockando 129

Ladyburn 89
Lagavulin 134, 144, 145, 151, 152
Landseer, Sir Edwin 2

Langholm 88
Laphroaig 43, 50, 134, 144, 145, 150, 151, 153
Linkwood 119
Littlemill 89
Lloyd George, David 34
Loch Fyne Whiskies 48
Lochhead 140
Lochindaal 140, 145, 148
Loch Katrine 89
Loch Lomond 74, 96
Lochrin 89
Lochside 97
Longmorn 52, 69, 119, 125
Longrow 136
Lossit, Islay 144

Macallan, The 16, 60, 119, 132
McCallum, Donald 140
Mac Donald 'Long John' 97
McDowall, R.J.S. 9
Macduff 97
Mackenzie Brothers 107
Mackenzie, Sir Compton 34, 39
Mackie, Peter 27, 152
Malt Mill 152
Man O' Hoy 114, 115
Mannochmore 119
Millburn 96, 102
Miltonduff 35, 119
Mitchell, J. & A. & Co. Ltd 136
Morrison Bowmore Distillers 47, 91, 147
Mortlach 118
Museum of Islay Life 17

Newton, Islay 144
Nikka Distillers 97
North British 76, 80, 81
North Port 97

Oban 97
Octomore Farm, Islay 144
Old Orkney 114

Old Pulteney 110
Old Vatted Glenlivet 20, 22
Ord 97, 106

Parkmore 118, 124, 132
Pattison, Robert 21
Pattison, Walter 21
Pattisons Ltd 21, 32, 83
Peel, Sir Robert 97
Pennant, Thomas 134, 144
Perth 16, 29, 35, 44, 85, 98, 99
Philip, HRH Prince 43
Pittyvaich 118
Port Dundas 89
Port Ellen 138, 144, 145, 149
Provanmill 89
Pulteney 37, 97, 110

Queen Anne 37, 41

Richardson, Sir Albert 35
Rieclachan 134, 136
Roderick Dhu 30
Rosebank 89, 90, 93
Rothes 28, 29, 118, 119, 126
Royal Brackla 96
Royal Lochnagar 97

St Magdalene 89, 90, 92
Scapa 97, 110, 112
Scotch Malt Whisky Society 9
Scotch Whisky Heritage Centre 9, 48
Scotia 137
Scottish Malt Distillers (SMD) 30, 34, 90
Seagram Distillers 35, 40, 75, 119
Sheriff & Co. 140
Smith, George 22, 118, 119, 128
Speyburn 119
Speyside 102

Speyside Cooperage 66, 67, 120
Springbank 91, 134, 136
Stein, Robert 13, 74, 149
Strathclyde 74, 89
Strathisla 40, 70, 119, 120, 125
Strathmill 119, 129
Stromness 114
Sunbury 89
Suntory 47, 147

Talisker 116, 145, 151
Tallant Farm, Islay 144
Tamdhu 129
Teacher, William & Sons Ltd 27, 53, 131, 132
Teacher's Highland Cream 131, 132
Teaninich 97
Tomatin 47, 96
Tormore 35, 40
Towser 99
Tullymet 25

United Distillers (UD) 35, 78, 89, 90, 93
United Distillers & Vintners (UDV) 35, 97, 101, 104, 106, 116, 118, 129, 130
Usher, Andrew 20, 22

Victoria, Queen 43

Walker, John & Sons Ltd 27
Whisky Galore 34, 39
White Horse 27, 152
White Horse Distillers Ltd 27
Whyte & Mackay Ltd 107
Williamson, Bessie 150
Wright & Greig Ltd 30

Yoker 89